Durorp-English Dictionary

Compiled by
Ekpe Inyang

Langaa Research & Publishing CIG
Mankon, Bamenda

Publisher:
Langaa RPCIG
Langaa Research & Publishing Common Initiative Group
P.O. Box 902 Mankon
Bamenda
North West Region
Cameroon
Langaagrp@gmail.com
www.langaa-rpcig.net

Distributed in and outside N. America by African Books Collective
orders@africanbookscollective.com
www.africanbookcollective.com

ISBN: 9956-790-94-X

© Ekpe Inyang 2013

DISCLAIMER

All views expressed in this publication are those of the author and do not necessarily reflect the views of Langaa RPCIG.

Purpose

Durorp is an interesting and linguistically distinct semi-Bantu or Bantoid language spoken by a minority group of people known as Bororp or people of the Kororp ethnic group. A part of this ethnic group inhabits the Southwestern part of Cameroon while the other occupies the Southeastern tip of Nigeria.

A minority group, Kororp has continued to suffer not only cultural and socio-economic shrinkage but also linguistic marginalisation characterised by an obvious erosion of some key elements of the language. Like any other language, however, Durorp has borrowings from languages such as Efik, Ejagham, and even English.

Like Kpewi Durorp which concentrates on the grammar of the language, Durorp-English Dictionary is aimed primarily at the linguistic emancipation of Kororp and at stimulating literary interests in the study and development of Durorp as a linguistic entity in particular and promotion of Durorp literature in general. To achieve this aim, this Dictionary has introduced quite a number of new but understandable words.

Abbreviations: The following abbreviations are used throughout the dictionary:
esp = especially
art = article
n = noun
pro = pronoun
adj = adjective
v = verb
aux.v = auxiliary verb
inf.v = infinite verb
adv = adverb
prep = preposition

conj = conjunction
inj = interjection or exclamation
lit = literal meaning
Eng. = English
Efi = Efik
Eja = Ejagham
Duk = Dukondokondo

Letters of the alphabet: a b ch d e f i j k m n o p q r s t u w y

Vowels: a e i o or u

Doubling of vowels: This is mostly done to indicate that the sound is longer than when the vowels were single, for example: aa ee ii oo oor uu

Consonants: b ch d f j k m n p q r s t w y

Varieties of Durorp: This dictionary is written based mainly on Dukorn, or the Ekorn variety of Durorp, except otherwise indicated.

Some Mathematical Language: Here are mathematical jargons and signs of some basic operations:

Operations		Signs	Examples	
Durorp	**English**		**Durorp**	**English**
Baba	Plus (Add)	+	Dio baba bunan	Ten plus three
Tor	Minus (Subtract)	-	Dio tor bunai	Ten minus four
Chuwere nta	Multiplied by	x	Dio chuwere nta orwan	Ten multiplied by two
Tuk a bikaim	Divided by	/	Dio tuk a bikaim biwan	Ten divided two
Bubura	Equals	=	Dio baba dio bubura	Ten plus ten equals

Aa

a (prep) at; in; to; from; on; by; that
e.g. 1. Nde a enor ndaikwai. *I am at home today.* (But note that the "a" is silent in the sentence since it is immediately followed by a word that begins with a vowel; this is the rule that applies without exceptions)
2. Nde a okum. *I am in the market.*
3. N nyi a ekpang. *I am going to the farm.*
4. N tunghi a Ekornganaku. *I am from Ekornganaku*
5. Or sou a butemini. *He/she is sitting on the floor.*
6. N ka nyi a uwan. *I shall go by canoe.*
7. Or beke a ngo a kpiya ingwha ingo. *He/she said that you should shut your mouth.*
(pro) you (singular); where is/are…?
e.g. 1. A ka quai? *Will you come?*
2. A reni ma. *You are not here.*
3. A na ror ibat nyor. *You have not understood that Math.*
4. A ri quai? *Won' you come?*
5. *M*mong a? *Where is he/she?*
aaikpai (n) a ring
aata utep (n) a hunter
aayang (n) a broom
a baikait baingo (pro) on your own; personally
e.g. 1. A yairi nkwet chai a baikait baingo? *Did you write this book on your own?*
2. A ka quai ma a baikait baingo? *Will come here personally ?*
abiabun (n) a needle; a syringe
e.g. 1. N chormi abiabun u kpaik eta emi. *I don't have a needle to stitch my clothes.*
2. Or yani u nuwa abiabun. *He/she doesn't like to take an injection.*
Aboong (n) (commonly spelt Abung) a Nigerian village of Kororp, found in the Oban District of Akamkpa Local Government Area, Cross River State
abubian (adj) lazy

e.g. Or re amamang abubian orne. *He/she is a typically lazy person.* (n) a lazy person
e.g. M biri de abubian. *I am not a lazy person.*
abuchor (n) an adulterer; an adultress
abudordor (n) [see also aburoror] a sage; an intellectual
abuka (n) a craftsman; an artist
abukei (adv) down
e.g. 1. Koom idiaii nyor abukei. *Put that cutlass down.*
2. Sa ungo abukei. *Sit you down.*
abukoi (n) a fisherman
abukormi (n) a builder
abukpaiki (n) a tailor; a seamstress
e.g. Ore abukpaiki. *He/she is a tailor/seamstress.*
abukpaan (n) a selfish-person
e.g. A re abukpan? *Are you a selfish-person?*
(adj) selfish
e.g. O re abukpan ornerom. *He is a selfish man.*
abumkpuk (n) a blind person
e.g. Or re abumkpuk. *He/she is a blind person.*

abunorngha (n) a sex maniac
aburoror (n) [see also abudordor] a sage; an intellectual
abuyairi (n) a writer; a teacher (a misnomer for)
anchormi (n) one who, or something that, lacks (see also anap)
adiagha [from Efi.](n) first daughter
a din da (adv) in the name of
e.g. Uyin umi u ka fore, a din da Jisors. Ure nyindior *My family will prosper, in the name of Jesus. Amen.*
adooroong (n) someone or animal with the propensity to bite; biter
e.g. Ornerom kwo ore adooroong. *This man is a biter.*
(adj) having the propensity to bite, biting
e.g. Ebia adooroong ndai. *This is a biting dog.*
adubam (adv) beside
e.g. N sou a dubam dumorng. *I am sitting beside him/her.*
adubung (n) a driver
e.g. A chorm adubung? *Do you have a driver?*

adukpak (n) a poor person
(adj) poor
a dunyor (adv) infront, ahead
aduret (adj) being prone to crying
(n) someone prone to crying
adutaina (n) a teacher (erroneously known as abuyairi)
afai (n) violence, brutality, ferocity, bestiality
e.g. Afai or noormi. *Violence is not good.*
afang (n) a wild, though recently domesticated vegetable, popularly known as "eru", used for preparing a rich West African soup
afarawa [from Eng.] (n) a flower
e.g. Afarawa quo or normi. *This flower is beautiful.*
aibon (pro) our; ours
aidiami (n) plan; strategy
e.g. 1. A chorm aidiami na aye ? *Do you have a plan with him/her?*
2. Ta chorma aidiami? *Do you already have a strategy ?*
aikpai (n) a rat; (figuratively) a thief
aikin (n) a joke

aimi (pro) my; mine (for singular possession)
e.g. 1. Quai enor aimi. *Come to my house.*
2. Chaap aimi ndior. *That is my meat.*
ainain (n) a track, a path, a route, a road; the way
aingo (pro) your; yours
e.g. Enor aingo ndai? *Is this your house?*
airaing...asik ...(conj) were it not for..., had it not been that...
e.g. 1. Ereng ngo asik... *Were it not for you...*
2. Ereng o quai asik...*Had it not been that he came...*
aiyain (n) place; point
ataip (n) exaggeration; overstatement; overstatement
ajigichak (n) large beads (usually a string worn round the waist, mostly by women in a traditional "school" such as fattening room after circumcision)
akam (n) a prayer; prayers
e.g. Borng akam ongo kporkpora daikwai. *Say your prayers everyday.*
akang (n) saltpeter (locally known as akanghwa, used for ground tobacco and for

cooking to prevent indigestion)
akangkang (n) a small, two-pronged metal gong
e.g. Meng or dor u koot akangkang ma. *Who knows how to beat the gong here.*
akara (n) bean cake, normally fried in bleached palm oil
akarasi (n) a glass
e.g. 1. Chang mmi akarasi. *Give me a glass.*
2. N ya u choorn mini a akarasi. *I like to drink water from a glass.*
akarasi enyin [from Efi.] (n) eyeglasses, spectacles, specs
e.g. Amene ormong or ya u korn akarasi enyin. *His/her father likes to wear spectacles.*
akemeen (n) a drunkard
e.g. Kpara nona mmung; o re akemeen. *Don't invite him/her; he/she is a drunkard.*
akikuku (n) a weakling, a person who has neither the strength to fight nor to do hard work.
e.g. Nik akikuku quor. *Leave that weakling.*
(adj) weak.

e.g. O re akikuku kor orne. *He/she is a weak person.*
akirimen [from Eng.] (n) agreement (usually a written one)
akitu (n) an extremely foolish person, an imbecile
(adj) the state of being extremely foolish
e.g. A re amamang atkitu. *You are an extremely foolish person.*
akpa (n) the number or position "first".
e.g. Mmi nde akpa a kras obon. *I am first in our class.*
(adj) the position first.
e.g. Mmi nde akpa orne u dion ma. *I was the first person to arrive here.*
akpakpat [from Efi..] (n) slippers
akpan (n) first son
e.g. Akpan omi o chain Beya. *My first son is called Beya.*
(adj) key, principal, most important.
e.g. Akpan a biain bu baqai mmi ma ere ukwen a enor a nwket. *The key thing that has brought me here is this discussion about the school.*

akpang (n) a brave person
(adj) brave.
e.g. Anya ore akpang orne. *Anya is a brave person.*
akpantornghor (n) the beginning
e.g. O biri de ma a akpantonghor. *He/she was not here at the beginning.*
(adj) coming at the beginning.
akpantornghor orne (n) a pioneer
e.g. N de akpantonghor orne a korsorwa kai. *I am a pioneer in this sitting.*
akpan ukwen (n) the truth
e.g. A tangha akpan ukwen? *Are you speaking the truth?*
(adj) true
e.g. U re akpan ukwen. *It is true.*
akparanja (n) a sword
Akpasang (n) an official but mistaken name for Orkpasang, a Cameroonian village of the Kororp ethnic group
akpatire (n) the last, the end, conclusion

e.g. A kpatire a biain,.... [lit. : *As a last thing*] *In conclusion,...*
(adj) the position or being last or the end.
e.g. I tap akpatire a ainain. *We have reached the end of the road.*
a kporkporor ini (adv) regularly, always
akwai (n) queen
akwana ini (adv) for a short time; for a short while
ama (n) mother; also aunt (usually going along with my/our; also meaning his/her mother)
e.g. 1. Chaina ama omi. *Greet my mother.*
2. Ama obon or reni enor. *Our mother is not in the house.*
3. Ama onyi duseeng. *His/her mother has travelled.*
a meng (pro) whose
e.g. Ebia a meng ndai? *Whose dog is this?*
ansiin (n) a hinge
ansiin ituum (n) a door hinge
amama (adj) a typical
e.g. Or re amama ornanaghi. *He/she is a typical liar.*

ama ama ama (n) maternal grandmother
ama ama amene (n) paternal grandmother
amamfaibairai (n) a liar
amaang (adj) [ofen used derogatorily] real, genuine, not fake or pretended; super
e.g. 1. N ka taina ngo amaang a biain. *I will teach you a real lesson.*
2. Amaang a dion ndai bor da be tonini ma a dodonghi daingo? *Is this a genuine gun or that made here behind your house?*
3. Kating a re ngo amaang orne! *You must be such a super human!*
ama orerei (n) grandmother
amang (adj) real; genuine; authentic
amang ukwen (n) the truth; honest truth
ambabadormorn (n) a consonant
ambabantainaniin (n) a pronoun
ambaka (adj) wet
e.g. A chang mmi ambaka eta chai? *You give me this wet clothes?*
ambap (n) immature type, especially of plantain and banana

ambei (adj) foolish
ambeet (adj) wide.
e.g. N yaani u chiork ambeet orkpa. *I don't like to swim in a wide river.*
ambekosai (n) a verb
ambia ibat (n) a person who carries the shoulders high, a proud person
ambiani (adj) lazy
e.g. Ambiani a kwen. *A lazy child.*
ambiap (adj) bad; ugly; dangerous
ambin (adj) black.
e.g. Ambin eta. *Black clothes*
ambini (adj) black.
e.g. Ambini a korsorwa. *A black chair.*
Ambin ita (n) a policeman (a euphemism for)
ambini orne (n) Black man
ambobi (adj) wide
e.g. Or chorm ambobi ikung. *He/she has a wide chest.*
ambot (adj) clean, pure
Ambot Ikung (n) [figuratively meaning one with a white or pure chest] God
ambori (adj) white
e.g. N ya ambori eta. *I like white clothes.*

amene (n) father; also auncle
e.g. Amene omi ndai. *This is my father.*
amene amene ama (n) maternal grandfather
amene amene amene (n) paternal grandfather
amene orerei (n) grand father
amfara (adj) fast, quick.
e.g. N kwaka amfafa kenweye. *I want a fast runner*
amfaibairai (adj) fond of lying, lying
e.g. Amfaibairai orne. *A lying person.*
amfebi (adj) light
e.g. Chang kwen kwor amfebi ekpa. *Give that child a light bag.*
aminkei (n) a relation or relative with whom one shares intimacy; a general term for: brother, sister, cousin
aminkei a buman (n) maternal cousin
aminkei a buwon (n) paternal cousin
aminkei oreonaton (n) sister
aminkei oreonerom (n) a brother
ampka (adj) pincers (of a crab or prawn)

amkpai kaibain (n) a tyrant
amkpam baikait (n) an arrogant person
amkpangha (adj) acidic
e.g. Amkpangha a sokoro. *An acidic orange.*
amkpani (adj) selfish
amkpeme bikaim (n) a security guard
amkpo (n) a traditional society in Kororp that represents the police force
amkporkor (adj) weak
e.g. Amkporkor onerom. *A weak man.*
amoi (n) cheating
e.g. Amamang amoi ndai. *This is real cheating.*
amorngheneukwen (n) a conjunction
amort munei (n) a treasurer
amuntorere (n) a narrator
anap (n) one who, or something that, lacks (see also anchormi)
anchau (adj) many; much
anchangdormorn (v) a vowel
anchangha (n) crayfish
anchanghi (adj) dry, thin, slim
anchor urum (n) spirit-masquerades in Kororp (regarded as children of

Amkpo), known more for their insulting nature, that come out by day or night and force people to lock their doors, as sign that something unusual has happned.

anchorma (n) owner

andan den (n) one blind in one eye

andeke (adj) dirty
e.g. Andeke eta. *Dirty clothes.*

andiara (adj) saltless, bland, insipid (of food)

andiom (adj) small

aandoon (n) a crab

andoon (adj) red

andooron (n) leprosy

andon nen (n) [figuratively] a bully, or person who frightens others into accepting deals against their will

andore (n) a variety of cocoyam usually cooked with the peelings and eaten by peeling and eating with either pepper-rich palm oil or palm oil-rich vegetable

andor benaii (n) a botanist

andor bumbet (n) a lawyer

andor buuka (n) a talent; an architect

andor dukuk da munaii (n) an accountant

andor ibat (n) a mathematician

andor ichap (n) a zoologist; a biologist

andor kaibain (n) a geographer

andor mbuk (n) a journalist

andor mbuk a kpain (n) a historian

andor muntort (n) an ornithologist

andor neeke na kpain (n) a folklorist

andor urum (n) a forester

andou (adj) heavy
e.g A chang quona kwen quo andou ekpa chor or nwam? *You gave this little child that heavy bag to carry?*

anduki (adj) dangerous; poisonous, venomous; deadly, lethal
e.g. 1. Anduki orne o dubi. *A dangerous person does not hide.*
2. Anduki enu ndai. *This is a poisonous snake.*
3. Anduki a borkor ba afai ndai. *These are deadly weapons.*

andum (adj) smelly.

e.g. Andum enor usaing chor? *That smelly toilet?*
aneke (adj) tasty, palatable
e.g. O sin u dia aneke a daria dai. *He/she has refused to eat this palatable food.*
aneu (adj) cold; calm
anferi (adj) thin; flat
e.g. A beke anferi a kababai kai? *Do you say this thin plank?*
anfiba (adj) tight; narrow
e.g. 1. Anfiba eta. *Tight clothes.*
 2. Anfiba ainain. *A narrow path.*
anghwa (n) a cat; (also figuratively), an agile person
anghwam donuna (n) a porter, a person whose service is to carry luggage
aning (conj) since
e.g. Aning mbe raing bai quai, mfina e deni. *Since they too have come there is no problem.*
ankai (adj) sour
e.g. A chang aye ankai a borkor bai? *You give him/her this sour food?*
ankain (n) a look-alike
e.g. Ankain ngo ndai. *This is your look-alike.*

ankaini (adj) cunning; clever
e.g. Ankeni a ornerom kwor?. *That cunning man?*
ankang (adj) big, fat, large
ankei (n) an abbreviated and a more intimate word for "aminkei"; a relative with whom one shares intimacy; a general term for: brother, sister, or cousin; sibling
ankoorere (adj) bending, twisting, winding
e.g. N yani u bung a ankoorere ainain. *I don't like to drive on a winding road.*
ankorn (adj) strong; hard; difficult.
e.g. 1. Ankorn onerom. *A strong man,*
2. Ankorn a kui. *A hard bone.*
3. Ankorn a duwom. *A difficult Job.*
ankoorn-buchor (n) an adulterer, an adultress
ankpaki (adj) poor.
e.g. Ankpaki onerom quor? *That poor man?*
ankuk munai (n) an accountant
ankuwi (adj) short

ankwak ukwen (n) troublesome, aggressive or antagonistic person e.g. Kwen quo or de atata ankwak ukwen. *This child is a typical troublesome person.*
(adj) troublesome, aggressive, antagonistic e.g. Kpara baquai ankwak ukwen a kwen ma. *Don't bring an aggressive child here.*
ankweu (adj) sharp e.g. Ankweu idiaii. *A sharp cutlass.*
ankworp (adj) soft (e.g. bone)
ankworor ukwen Orbasi (n) preacher, Pastor
anhao! (inj) an expression of fortune or good news
anning baikait (n) a proud person
(adj) proud
anorm (adj) beautiful; good e.g. Anorm aton omorng quor? *That his beautiful wife?*
ansaka (adj) torn
ansang (n) a frog
ansara (adj) thin e.g. Nwam ansara iworn ingo nyor bari ma. *Carry those thin legs of yours out of here.*
ansaiki (adj) bitter
ansai nookon (n) a farmer
ansime (adj) stupid e.g. A ba ansime kwen quo ngha ankuk munei? *You employ this stupid child as an accountant?*
ansiya (adj) stupid; dull
ansuka (adj) bushy e.g. Meng or chorm ansuka ekpang chai? *Who has this bushy farm?*
antakchior (conj) so, for that reason
antak a (conj) because, because of; sake
1. N kwoba aye antak a o biri fara dik. *I beat him/her because she did not return early*
2. Jises or kwa antak a aibon. *Jesus died for our sake.*
antadunghor (n) firstborn
antaina ainain (n) a guide
antaina baikait (adj) a showy person
antainakochok (n) an interjection
antainaniin (n) a noun
antainarangosai (n) an adverb
antainarangure (n) an adjective

atainaiyainore (n) a preposition
a ntak (conj) sake
e.g. M baima a ntak engo. *I accepted for your sake.*
antenghe (adj) soft (e.g. rope)
antorbor (adj) muddy
antort (adj) hot.
e.g. Antort a dion du? *This hot fire?*
antort esin (n) ill-temprered or bad-tempered person
(adj) ill-temprered; bad-tempered; cantankerous
antort inghwa (n) a highly convincing liar
antortort (n) a hot drink
anturi (adj) blunt.
e.g. Anturi idiaii i noormi a dusei. *A blunt cutlass is not good for slashing.*
anwa (n) a cat (a pussy cat)
anwam baikait (n) a proud person
anyam (n) a Kororp masquerade dressed in banana leaves; a male name of Kororp
ataim (n) a traditional society that represents barren people
anyeng (n) an absess
anyenghe (adj) sweet
e.g. Anyenghe orkem quo, a sin u men? *This sweet palm wine, you refuse to drink?*
anyiri (adj) tall; long
e.g. N ya anyiri orne. *I like a tall person.*
anyiri ini (adv) a long time; time immemorial
anyir iwoorn (n) [lit.: long feet] a trousers
anyop bene (n) a deceiver
a quai (v) [lit.: "Have you come?"] welcome (for a visitor)
arangha (adv) the way; how
e.g. Ket arangha n sai. *Observe the way I do it/ See how I do it.*
aranghaquo (adv) now, right now, at this moment; currently; immediately
are (v) [lit.: "Are you there?"] good afternoon or good evening
a rik (v) welcome [lit.: "Have you returned?"] (for a resident)
arukanyor (n) [from Eja.] a beard
arum (n) a sperm; sperms
asaam (n) a spear
asen (art) the
e.g. Orne asen a?

Where is the person?
asik (adj) [also Eja.] not, it's not; but for
e.g. 1. Mmorng asik. *It's not him/her.*
2. Airaing mmorng asik kun mbiri yeu orkpa quor. *But for him/her I would not have crossed that river.*
ata (v) were…alright
e.g. Ata mmorng kun ta o buki. *Were he alright he would have been up by now.*
antakchior (conj) thereore; thus; for that reason
e.g. N na fikiri dor kwa a chana u sai, antakchior n dorni unyangha a n ka chang ngo. *I don't really know what you plan to do, for that reason I don't know what help to give you*
atata *(adv)* really, typical
e.g. O re atata kwen a bak. *He/she is really a young child.*
atoon (n) wife; also simply meaning his wife
e.g. 1. Atoon orne ndior. *That is someone's wife.*
2. Atoon omi ndai. *This is my wife.*
3. Atoon ormorng ndai? *Is this his wife?*

ata utaip (n) a hunter
awaiwait (n) cartilage, soft bone - commonly known as biscuit bone
e.g. Atoon omi orya u dia awaiwait. *My wife likes to eat soft bone.*
awawa [from Efi.] (n) sea waves; tide; high tide
awewet (v) a pest, pests (especially animals of the rodent group)
e.g. Awewet or chaawi kpai a dusai du. *There are too many pests in this village/community.*
Ayaang (n) a Kororp female name
a yaini (v) [lit.: *have you (sing.) woken up?*] good morning
ayaya na ayani (v) like it or not
e.g. Ayaya na ayani, a chorm u taba mmi aranghaquo. *Like it or not, you have to follow me now.*
aye (pro) him, her
e.g. Be chang aye din antak a orkporsorng a dumeen. *They have given him a name because of excessive drinking.*
ayikwai (adv) nowadays; these days; present generation

e.g. Mini mu norba kpai ayikwai. *The rain is falling too much nowadays.*

ayo (n) A Kororp moonlight dance or performance that involves males and females

ayoo! (inj) an expression of praise for a good performance

ayoyo (n) [from Inani Ayoyo or Ayoyo Rock], a euphemism for greatness, magnificence; a great person, a great

e.g. Nke are ayoyo, kpara numene mmi. *Even if you were a great, don't try it on me.*

Bb

ba (v) take; own; marry; use
e.g.1. Duwom dor du ka ba ngo ini iwang? *How long will that job take you?*
2. Ba ekpa chor cha a kpemi mmi. *Own the bag you borrowed from me.*
3. Or kwaka u ba mmi. *He/she wants to marry me.*
4. Ba munork mor. *Use that salt.*
(adv) that; what
e.g. 1. Biain ba N kwaka ndai. *This is the thing that I want/have been searcing for.*
2. N ning biain ba N kwaka. *I have seen what I want/have been searcing for.*
(prep) of
e.g. Ben ba onerom quor ndai. *These are the children of that man.*
(adv) since
e.g M ba mana N na ning enyi a mini. *Since I was born I have not seen a hippopotamus.*
(conj) before
e.g. Chooya a ba quai. *Bathe before you come.*
baaba (v) lean against.
e.g. Baba a dubut. *Lean against the wall.*
baabi (v) peel off or detach continuously (especially objects with flat surfaces); palpitate
e.g. 1. Kpara baabi coong ka kainaii kor. *Don't peel off the bark of that tree.*
1. Kpara sai esin e baabi mmi. *Don't make my heart to palpitate.*
baabi esin (v) panic
baabiri (v) palpitating
baakara (v) make wet
e.g. Kwen kwor or baakara mmi kpat. *That child has wet me completely.*
baakpak (n) poor people; the poor
e.g. Nyangha bakpak. *Help the poor.*
baama (n) mothers
e.g. Baama baibon ndai. *These are our mothers.*
baat (v) stand; halt
e.g. Baat mandior. *Stand/halt there.*
baat taak (v) stall, stalled; halt, halted
baba (v) add; follow behind; born after; support; second
babi (v) peel off, detach (done quickly, especially to objects with flat surfaces)

baboong (n) the people of Aboong
babuka (n) craftsmen; architects; artists, talents
babukoi (n) fishermen
babukpaan (n) selfshish people
ba buqun (v) get or become pregnant
e.g. Or ka ba buqun. *She will become pregnant.*
(adj) pregnant
e.g. Or ba buqun. *She is pregnant.*
bacha (pro) people's
e.g. Ben ba bacha. *People's children.*
badukpak (n) poor or impoverished people
(adj) poor; impoverished
bafat (n) twins
bai (pro) these; these ones
e.g. Ben baimi bai ka yeu uromo umbe. *These my children will pass their exams.*
(v) praise; congratulate; commend; worship; extol; honor
e.g. U normi u bai ben be nuu u but ainain. *It is good to commend children who aim for success.*
baibon (pro) our; ours (for plural possessions)
e.g. 1. Borkor baibon ndai. *These are our things.*
2. Bene baibon ndai. *These are our people.*
baikait (n) body
baikait a? (v) how are you?
baikait baingo a? (v) how are you?
baikait baingo (pro) yourself
baima (v) accept, accepted; agree, agreed; admit, admitted; consent, consented; believe, believed
e.g. 1. M baima. *I accept/I have accepted*
2. M baima a Omuna Obasi. *I believe in the Lord God.*
baimi (pro) my; mine (for plural possessions)
e.g. Ben baimi ndai. *These are my children.*
bain (v) put an injunction
bainaii (n) trees; sticks
e.g. N tou ekese a bainaii a dokon daimi. *I have planted many trees in my farm.*
baingo (pro) your, yours (singular pronoun for plural possessions)
e.g. 1. Borkor baingo ndai? *Are these your things?*

2. Bcken baingo be quai. *Your visitors have come.*
baikpiya (n) orphans
baira (v) light; illuminate
e.g. Mbork, baira dion dor. *Please, light that lamp/fire.*
bairere (v) raise, raise up; take up; promote; exalt
bairuk (adj) another (for nouns beginning with "be", "ba", "bor" or "bo"); some
e.g. 1. Borkor bairuk ndai. *Here are other things.*
2. Bene bairuk bai kaik tatana kor. *Some people have gone that way.*
baisit (n) babysitters
bait (v) climb especially a tree, a hill or mountain; ascend, rise
e.g. e.g. A keme u bait kenaii kor? *Can you climb that tree?*
baisin (n) livers
bak (adj) fresh; young
e.g.1. I kwaka chaap a bak. *I want fresh meat.*
2. O re kwen a bak. *He/she is a young child.*
baka (adj) wet, drenched
e.g. Ita nyi i baka. *These clothes are wet.*
baka baka (adj) soaking wet

e.g. O dioni quai na ita i baka baka. *He came in with clothes wet.*
bakaka (n) giant pangolins (a specified number of)
bakang (adj) quills (a specified number of)
e.g. N chorm bakang ba chioop dio. *I have ten porcupine quills.*
bakani (n) ghosts, aparisions; ancestors
bakara (v) to turn oneself or someone round in a lying position
bakara...inum (v) betray
e.g. Ntangha chang ngo u tibe aranghaquo, nnangha kpara bakara mmi inum. *I am telling you what is happening now, but don't betray me.*
bakikuku (n) weaklings
e.g. A koona bakikuku bai a ben? *You refer to these weaklings as children?*
bakpa (n) a Durup name for Ejagham or Banyangi people
e.g. I chorm uben na bakpa. *We have a boundary with the Ejagham.*
bakpain (n) ancient people; ancestors
e.g. Bakpain be taina ibon ndai, kun I biri dor. *It is*

the ancestors that have taught us like this, we would not have known.
bakpak (n) forked sticks, two-pronged sticks used for holding up a pole or poles (a specified number of)
bambekosai (n) verbs
bambin ita (n) policemen (a euphemism for)
ba meng (pro) whose
e.g. Buria ba meng ndai? *Whose yams are these?*
bameng (pro) who (in plural)
e.g. Bameng ndior? *Who are those?*
bami (v) open especially a bag, or anything structured like a bag, or mouth.
e.g. Kpara bami ingwha ingo daing. *Don't open your mouth again.*
baminkei (n) relations—brothers, sisters, ousins
baminkei ba buman (n) maternal cousins
bambabadormorn (n) consonants
baminkei ba buwon (n) paternal cousins
bamkpeme bikaim (n) security guards
bamorngheneukwen (n) conjunctions

ban (v) sex
bana (v) get engaged in sex (for several people to)
banana (n) banana (tree or especially the green fruits)
banbabantainaniin (n) promouns
banchangdormorn (n) vowels
bandor benaii (n) botanists
bandor buuka (n) talents
bandor dukuk da muniei (n) accountants
bandor ibat (n) mathematicians
bandor ichap (n) zoologists; biologists
bandor kaibain (n) geographers
bandor mbuk (n) journalists
bandor muntort (n) ornithologists
bandor mbuk kpain (n) historians
bandor neeke na kpain (n) folklorists
bandor urum (n) foresters
bangha (adj) about, concerning
e.g Nke mbuk e bangha aye? *Not even news about him/her?*
bankpantornghor ba

bene (n) pioneers
e.g. I re bakpantornghor ba bene a kormbaani quo. *We are pioneers in this company.*
bang (v) serves someone (you) right.
e.g. A bang. *It serves you right*
bangha (inf.v) about; concerning
e.g. 1. Ufaikere quu u bangha mmung? *What is this argument about?*
2. Erequa a kpanghi biain bu bangha mmi, num be kona mmi. *If you hear anything concerning me, send for me.*
(conj) in regard to; involving
banghwam donuna (n) porters, people whose service is to carry luggage
bangworo (n) the people of Ngworo
bani (v) become/get well, became:got well; recover from an illness, recovered from an illness
e.g. Akam omi or de a ngo afara bani. *My prayer is for you to get well soon.*
bankain (n) look-alikes

bankondup (n) the people of Nkondup
bansai nokon (n) farmers
e.g. Bata utaip be chau kpai bansai nokon a dusai du. *Hunters are more in number than farmers in this village.*
bantak (n) insects (a specified number of)
bantaina (n) teachers
bantaina ainain (n) guides
bantainakochok (n) interjections
bantainaniin (n) nouns
bantainarangosai (n) adverbs
bantainarangure (n) adjectives
batainaiyainore (n) prepositions
bantem (v) companions; colleagues; ounterparts; [implied] others
e.g. Bantem be tornghor etoowa. *Others have started plantings.*
baquai (v) bring; brought
e.g. Baquai mini mor ma. *Bring that water here.*
bari (v) leave.
e.g. Bari aranghaquo. *Leave now.*
bari chang (v) forgive, forgave, forgiven; pardon, pardoned

e.g. M bari chang mboon. *I have forgiven you.*
bari mandio chang (v) forgive, pardon.
e.g. Bari mandio chang mmi. *Forgive me.*
baria (adj) yams (a specified number of)
e.g. Baria bawang a dewe a munaii mor? *How many yams have you bought for that amount?*
batake (n) a ladder
basak (adj) rattles (musical instruments; (a specified number of)
batan ba diat (n) jaw bones
batana (n) sides, areas, quarters
bata utaip (v) hunters
baton (n) women
e.g. Nik borom na batom be simini. *Let men and women assemble.*
ba ufen (v) suffer, suffered
e.g. Be ba ufen kpai. *They have suffered too much.*
bawa (n) short-snouted crocodiles (a specified number of)
bayo (n) people, especially of doubtful character (usually followed by be [these] or bor [those])

e.g. Bayo bor nyenene? *Those people again?*
be (n) they
e.g. 1. Be ka sai nning ko be bait tap ma? *What will they do in order to climb up to this point?*
2. Be re mmang? *Where are they?*
bebe (v) fly, flew; fly away, flew away; jump, jumped
e.g. 1. Itort nyor i kemeni u bebe. *That bird cannot fly.*
2. A keme u bebe ikit? *Can you jump (do) high jump?*
bebere (v) cause to fly away; realease (a bird)
e.g. 1. Kpara bebere itort imi. *Don't cause my bird to fly away.*
2. Bebere itort nyor. *Release that bird.*
beebi (v) fly or jump repeatedly; flying
e.g. Kwen itort nyor I tornghor u beebi. *That nestling has started flying.*
beebiri (v) flying
e.g. Muntort my beebiri a echong a dubut. *Birds are flying in the sky.*
beet (adj) wide
e.g. Orkpa, bu beet! *The river, so wide!*

(v) mud (the walls of) a house; that is make the walls of a traditional house by plastering the framework with mud

e.g. Batoon be dor u beet enor. *Women know how to mud a house.*

befain (n) people; the people of; supporters; team members; acquaitances; relatives

e.g. Befain aimi ndai. *Here are my people.*

bee (v) are not; have not; will not

e.g. 1. Bee reni ma. *They are not here.*

2. Bee choormi nkwet a dono. *They don't have identity cards/passports.*

3. Bee ri quai. *They will not come.*

beeri neen (adj) naïve (esp. to the point of trusting people with whom one is not familiar)

e.g. Kwen ongo or beeri neen kpai. *Your child is too naïve.*

beet neen (v) be naïve (esp. to the point of trusting people with whom one is not familiar)

e.g. Kpara beet neen. *Don't be naïve.*

beghe (v) arrive, arrived (usually a person or people awaited); sail ashore, sailed ashore (usually a canoe, boat or ship)

e.g. 1. Baifain ba Ekorn be beghe. *The people of Ekon have arrived.*

2. Uwan ungo ta u beghe. *Your canoe has sailed ashore.*

bei (v) belch; behave foolishly

e.g. 1. Meng or bei ndior? *Who belched like that?*

2. Kpara bei. *Don't behave foolishly.*

(adj) foolish

e.g. Kating a bei? *Are your foolish?*

bek (v) tell, told; say, said; instruct, instructed; ask, asking, asked

e.g. 1. Bek mbe a ta N kwe. *Tell them that I have come.*

2. Akwaka u bek mmung? *What do you want to say.*

3. Bek mbe kwa be ka sai. buki baat. *Instruct them what to do.*

4. M bek (mbe) ma be yen. *I have asked them to go.*

beke (v) tell, telling, told; say, saying, said; instruct, instructing, instructed; ask, asking, asked
e.g. 1. M beke ngo mmung? a) *What are you telling them? b) What did I tell you?*
2. A beke mmung? a) *What are you saying. b) What did you say?*
3. M bek mbe kwa be ka sai. *I have instructed them what to do.*
4. M beke ma be yen. *I am asking them to go.*
beken (n) strangers; visitors
e.g. Bu biri de daing beken ma. *You are no longer strangers here.*
bekorn (n) the people of Ekorn
bekornganaku (n) the people of Ekornganaku
bekork (n) a bed
e.g. A rere a bekork kpat aranghakwo? *You are in bed up until now?*
bekorn (n) the people of Ekon
bekpiya (n) orphans
bembe (pro) their; their (for plural possessions)
e.g. Borkor bembe ndai. *These are their things.*

bemorng (pro) his/her/it; his/hers/its (for plural possessions)
e.g. Borkor bemorng ndai. *These are his/her things.*
bemboon (pro) your, yours (in plural)
e.g Borkor bemboon ndai. *These are your things.*
ben (n) children
ben ba bak (n) babies
ben ba sokoro (n) limes
ben ba buman (n) maternal nephews or nieces
ben ba buwon (n) paternal nephews or nieces
ben ba enor (n) servants
ben ba opko (n) assistants to a hunter or hunters responsible for carrying the meat and other items
benborchorn (n) young children
e.g. Bayo be bere atata benborchorn. *These people are really very young children.*
(adj) young; youth (in plural)
bene (n) people
bene ba enork (n) soldiers
bene ba ita (n) law enforcement officers

bene ba ukut (n) the marginalised; the disadvantaged; the underprivileged; the deprived; the needy

benghee (v) branch; branch off
e.g. N ka benghee enor a mborya omi. *I will branch to my buddy's house.*

bere (v) are; fine (response to "baikait a?"), e.g. nouns that begin with "ba", "be" and "bo" go with "bere"
(adj) available

berere (v) widen, open wide

beruk (adj) another, other (for nouns beginning with "be"
e.g. Bene beruk bere ndor. *There are other people there.*

beya (v) they like, they love or they are in support
(n) male name meaning the same as the verbal expression

beyani (v) they don't like, they don't love or they are not in support of
(n) female name that means the same as the verbal expression

bia (v) carry

biaan (v) break (into pieces, e.g. a bottle)
e.g. A kpara biaan akarasi kwor. *Don't you break that glass.*
(n) medicine
e.g. Kwen quo or yani u ba bian. *This child does not like to take medicine.*

biaan ba dayawa (n) love charm

biabi (adj) bad

biai (v) split, splitting (by hitting on the ground e.g. wood); clap
e.g. 1. Biai imet nyor a chang mmi. *Split that wood for me.*
2. Biai ibor bu chang aye. *Clap hands for him/her.*

biai ibor (v) clap hands, applaud, cheer

bia ibat (v) carry your shoulders high, be proud

biak (v) break many things; to crack (e.g. egusi)
e.g. 1. Or biak bukpeme. *He/she has broken the bottles.*
2. Aton omi or biak ikon *My wife has cracked egusi.*

biaam (n) medium sized fish with small mouths and something like craw-craw on their noses; hence the pidgin name of "craw-craw nose"

bian (n) zincs, corrugated roofing sheets

bianini (adj) lazy
e.g. Kwen quor or bianini *That child is lazy.*

biantum (adv) unawares; abruptly
e.g. 1. O kuba mmi biantum, nkwor u sai or bieni mmi a bukei. *He/she took me unawares, which is he/she threw me down.*
2. Mini mu wiriri biantum, nkendior N keme u toi ita imi a utung ko I de baaka. *The rain poured abruptly, but I was able to remove my clothes from outside before they got wet.*

biain (n) something; a thing; a lesson
e.g. 1. Biain bu reni enor. *There is nothing in the house.*
2. A ka dia biain? *Will you eat something?*
3. N ka taina ngo biain. *I will teach you a lesson.*

biain ba afai (n) a weapon

biain ba durup (n) a secret

biain ba mbet (n) contraband goods
e.g. Norborn ne de biain bam bet. *Cartridges are contraband goods.*

biap (v) be bad
e.g. Aning bu kemeni u toro kwa N sai, N ka tornghor u biab. *Since you cannot commend my I am doing, I shall start to be bad.*

bien (v) throw, threw, thrown; throw away, threw away, thrown away; pour, poured; pour away, poured away; dispose, disposed of

bien…a bukei (v) (figuratively) let down, disappoint
e.g. Kpara bien ibon a bukei. *Don't disappoint us/Don't let us down.*

biere (v) judge; pass a judgment

bifokoro (n) lungs

bifu (n) herbs used especially for medicine

bii (v) there is no, are not; have not; will not
e.g. 1. Bikum bii reni daing. *There is no bikum again.*
2. Biini bii chawi daing. *Ants are not many again.*
3. Tornghor tornhor ini nyor, biini bii na quai

daing ma. *Since that time, ants have not come here again.*

bika (v) to shake (e.g. object including a human); jingle (e.g. a bell)

e.g. 1. Erequa a bika kainaii kor echimi e ka wiriri. *If you shake that tree the fruits will pour.*

2. Bika nkarika chor ko be tire kaichim. *Jungle the bell so that they stop the noise.*

bikaim (n) parts, portions, spots

e.g. Tuk chaap vhor a bikaim biwan. *Share that meat into two parts.*

bikondokondo (n) the people of Ikondokondo

bikum (n) a solitary masquerade, unaccompanied by humans, that announces the harvest of plums each year and marks the end of Efeng festival

bikuut (n) ramshackles (buildings near collapse); a bad omen

e.g. A Kororp u re bikuut u nenene na okongha. *In Kororp, it is a bad omen to encounter a chameleon.*

biim (v) pull continuously, drag

biini (n) ants

biinghene (v) roll (continuously over a distance, especially a log)

e.g. Nik i biinghene kikukum ki. *Let us roll this stump.*

biinghini (v) roll; wriggle

e.g. N ya u biinghini a kornorngha kaimi. *I like to roll in my bed.*

biiri (aux. v) would have

e.g. M biiri quai. *I would have come.*

bima (v) pull (once or briefly)

bimbe (pro) their; theirs (for plural possessions)

e.g. Bian biimbe ndai. *These are their basins/sheets of zinc.*

bimi (pro) my; mine (for plural possessions)

e.g. Bian bimi ndior. *Those are my basins/sheets of zinc.*

bimorng (pro) his/her/it; his/hers/its (for plural possessions)

e.g. Bian bimorng ndai. *These are his/her basins/sheets of zinc.*

bin (v) linger around

e.g. A rere u bin ma? *You are still lingering around here?*
binghebinghene (adj) low; lowly
bini (v) sigh; linger round; tranform into a totem
e.g. 1. A bini mmung ma? *Why are you ligering round here?*
2. A sai N ka bini ekwe aranghaquo. *If you joke I will transform into a leopard right now.*
binini (v) sighing
e.g. A binini mmung? *Why are you sighing?*
bingha (v) go down, descend
e.g. A ka keme u bingha orbereng quor? *Will you be able to descend that valley?*
binghene (v) lower; depose; turn down espcecially the volume of sound or the intensity of light; reduce/ bring down/cut down (the cost or price of)
e.g. 1. Be binghene aye kabara. *They have reduced his rank*
2. Be binghene aye. *He has been diposed.*
3. Binghene utoninkang quor. *Turn down that lamp.*
4. Mbork, binghene okum. *Please, cut down the cost/price.*
binghene baikait (v) condescend; be humble
e.g. O sin u binghene baikait u chorma nneme na baifain ba duwom bemorng. *He has refused to condescend to have a dialogue with his workers.*
bingo (pro) you, yours (singular pronoun, for plural possessions)
e.g. Bian bingo ndai. *These are you basins/sheets of zinc.*
binun (n) bile
bioi (v) hire; use, utilise, exploit
e.g. 1. Bioi mbe u sai duwom duwom dungo. *Hire them to do your work.*
2. M bioi seng idiai ingo u ne ekpang aimi. *I sometimes use your cutlass to clear my farm.*
3. Or bioi ifiork ibon u sai dowom dor. *He/she exploits our technique to do the job.*
(adj) cold

e.g Bioi bu nu nne. *I feel cold.*
(n) a cold
e.g. Bioi bu kuba nne. *I have a cold.*
biook (n) brows
biook ba nenn (n) eye brows
e.g. N ya ansuka a biook ban en bungo bor. *I love those bushy eye brows of yours.*
bioong (n) shells (of tortoises, snails or nuts); peelings (of banana, plantain, cassava); skins or hides (of animals), barks (of trees)
bioong ba inghwa (n) lips
biop (n) porcupines
bire (inf. v) are e.g. words that begin with "bi", including "bian" which is the plural of "tian", excepting "bian" which means medicine", go with "bire"
biri (inf. v) does not; did not
e.g. M biri quai. *I did not come.*
biri de (inf.v) am not, is not, are not, was nor, were not
e.g. M biri de orne a nsu. *I am not a liar.*
biruk (adj) another, other (for nouns that begin with "bi"
e.g. Biini biruk bi dion. *Other ants have entered.*
bito (adv) a while ago
e.g. O quai ma bito. *He/she came here a while ago.*
bitum (n) huts
e.g. I ning ekese a bitum urum qu.*We have seen many huts in this forest.*
biunn (n) axes
biyobiyoyo (n) two masquerades during efeng that reflect loving couples; (figuratively) a loving couple or loving couples.
e.g. Onerom quor na aton omorng be re amamang a biyobiyoyo. *That man and his wife are a typical loving couple.*
bobobiri (n) sheets (specified number) of paper
boduki [also boruki] (n) cruel, evil, wicked or dangerous persons; villains; criminals
bofi (n) mortgage
e.g. Or kwaka u chang ita imorng a bofi. *He wants*

to give out his clothes in mortgage.
boi (v) take care of; bring up, especially a family
e.g. A keme u boi enor? *Can you bring up a family?*
bok (v) mould
e.g. Bok bunang Bor. *Mould that fufu.*
bokit (n) head-tie; head scarf
bokor ba urum (n) natural resources; species
boma (v) spread out, for example, a mat; make a bed
e.g. Boma uboong quor ma. *Spread out that mat here.*
bonum (n) elders; the old
bonumwok (n) red colobus monkeys (a specified number of)
e.g. Bai buut bonumwok dio. *They have shot ten red colobus monkeys.*
booma (v) usually derogatorily used as command for a huge person or large animal to lie prostrate
boonghene (v) wander around aimlessly; wandering
boonum (n) elders

e.g. Kpono boonum. *Respect elders.*
bondru (n) [from Eng] a bail especially of zinc
e.g. N ka deu bondru a tian orwaan. *I will buy two bails of zinc.*
bononoki (n) drunkards
e.g. N yani u wana na bononoki. *I don't like to associate with drunkards.*
bor (conj) or; whether
e.g.1. A kwaka nkwet bor inaii a nkwet? *Do you want a book or a pen?*
2. N doorni bor or ka quai. *I don't know whether he will come.*
(pro) those; those ones
e.g. Ubangha ben baingo bor, ta i chorma aidiami u kpe mbe munaii. *Concerning those your children, we have a plan to pay them some money.*
(prep) that
e.g. Biain bor? *That thing?*
bora (adj) clean; become clean
e.g. 1. Usan qwor u bora? *Is the plate clean?*
2. O bora yen. *He/she has become clean a little/bit.*
bori (adj) clean
e.g. Ita nyor i bori? *Are those clothes clean?*
(v) made

e.g. Meng o bori ngo? *Who made you?*
bork (v) plait (hair); weave, especially a traditional cage of palm fronds
e.g. 1. Mmung a yani u bork nin ningo? *Why don't you like plaiting your hear?*
2. N doni u bork dubeng. *I don't know how to weave a cage.*
borkor (n) things, items; property
borkor ba afai (n) weapons
borkor ba afai be keme u dima kabain (n) weapons of mass destruction
borkor ba kpain (n) artefacts
borkor bokum (n) articles of trade
borkorkoi (n) kingfishers; (figuratively) skilled fishermen
borkoryorng (n) the people of Orkoryorng
borkpasang (n) the people of Orkpasang
borkporkobait (n) the people of Okporkobait
borl (n) (from Eng.) ball
borng (v) pray

borng akam (v) say prayers
bornorngi (n) maggots (a specified number of)
bornoort (n) nails (finer or toe nails) (a specified number of)
bornornoormi (n) dancers
borom (n) men
boror (v) answer, answered; respond, responded, reply, replied
e.g. A na boror mmi a kwa nwingha ngo. *You have not respeended to what I hinted you.*
boorng (v) wait, wait for
e.g. Boorng ibon I seng kiroorng. *Wait for us to travel together.*
bororp (n) people of Kororp
bortor (n) singers
boruki [also boduki] (n) cruel, evil, wicked or dangerous persons; villains; criminals
borsorwa (n) chairs, sofas (a specified number of)
bot (v) make; create; manufacture; invent
e.g. Orne or kemeni u bot orne. *A man cannot create a man.*
bowa (v) waste, spoil, destroy, damage; spend

bowa ini (v) waste time, delay, hesitate, tarry, procrastinate

bowowomi (n) hard-working people
e.g. U normi u kpe bowowomi kpai babian. *It is good to pay hardworking people more than lazy people.*

bu (pro) you (the plural); this; this one
e.g. 1. Bu re. [lit.:*Are you there?*] *Good afternoon / Good evening.*
2. Bu ka quai? *Will you come?*
3. Ngo biain bu. *You this thing.*
(adv) so many, so much
e.g. 1. Bene, bu chau. *People, so many.*
2. Daria, bu chau! *Food, so much!*

buba (n) blouse

bubam (n) pockets

bubanana (n) bananas (the trees)

bubaabi esin (v) palpitation

bubaii (n) ugliness

bubeb (n) storms
e.g. Ini a bubeb ndai. *This is a period for storms.*

bubeet neen (n) naïvity (esp. to the point of trusting people with whom one is not familiar)

bubia (n) dogs; pottos

bubian (n) laziness

bubiap emana (n) bad behaviour

bubiap esin (n) bad-heartedness

bubobi (n) width

bubobiri (n) sheets (of paper)

bubon (pro) our; ours

buboop (n) wings

bubot (n) cleanliness

bubura (inf.v.) mean or means
e.g. Uta bu biain bubura nning? *This sort of thing means what?/What does this sort of thing mean?*

buchichik (n) extreme fright or fear
e.g. Buchichik bu kuba mi ini a N ning ebeng or dia chaap koorp. *I was gripped by fright when I saw the way he was eating meat raw.*

buchor (n) snails; adultery (in plural)

buchoror (n) rattles worn round the ankles and used for dancing to produce the sound

buchooya (n) the act of bathing; a bath

e.g. I nyi buchooya. *Let's go for a bath.*
buchoya koron (n) fairness of the skin
budia inwha (n) taunting, boasting aimed, at overwhelming an oponent or oponents
e.g. Ntem ongo quo orya budia inwha. *This your friend is so fond of taunting.*
budiara (adv) saltless (of food); bland
e.g. N yani u dia borkor budiara. *I don't like eating food saltless.*
buroror (n) [see also buroror] knowledge, understanding; cleverness; intelligence; shrewdness; wisdom
bufebi (n) lightness; buoyancy
bui (v) stir continuously; prepare food by chopping into smaller pieces with the use of a small mortar stick, for instance cocoyams into a kind of pudding; pollute (especially water)
1. e.g. Bui erop chor. *Stir that soup.*
2. Bui ekon idio. *Prepare ekon idio (or cocoyam pudding)*
3. Kwen quor or ka bui mini mor. *That child will pollute that water.*
(n) bones
e.g. Bubia buy a bui. *Dogs like bones.*
bui bui (adj) bony; skinny, thin, emaciated; all skin and bones
e.g. O ki re bui bui. *He/she is now all skin and bones.*
bui ba itang (n) ribs
buk (v) tell, told, inform, informed, report, reported
e.g. Buk ibom u tibe. *Tell us what happened.*
bukai (n) sour, sour taste feeling of acidic taste
bukaina (n) resemblance
bukaini (n) cunning; cleverness
bukaka (n) giant pangolins
bukam (n) plantains (the trees)
bukang (n) quills
bukei (n) ground, land, earth
bukeme (n) embers, hot charcoal
bukemika [from Eng.] (v) chemicals
bukere (v) help someone or something up from a lying position;

rescusitate or bring back to life
buki (v) stand, stand up; wake, wake up; resurrect
bukikere (n) thoughts; ideas
bukiichin [from Eng.] (n) kitchens
bukorma (n) the act of rubbing the body with oil
bukormi (n) the art of building; the style of tying
bukormbani (n) companies
bukorn baikait (n) strength; good health e.g. 1. A chorm mmung bukorn baikai ko a kwaka u nwam andou a donuna dai? *What strength do you have that you want to carry this heavy load?*
2. Orbasi or chang mmi bukorn baikait. *God has given me good health.*
bukorn dono (n) stubbornness; obstinacy
bukorn esin (n) bravery; perseverance, endurance, stoicism, courage
bukorn nen (n) smartness; ability of not being easily cheated or deceived
bukot dono (n) headache; trouble
bukon kiro (n) difficulty of behaviour, naughtiness
bukpa (n) bags
bukpaan (n) selfishness
bukpaai (n) combs
bukpai (n) rings
bukpaikaibain (n) tyranny
bukpaiki (n) sewing
bukpak (n) forked sticks, two-pronged sticks used for holding up a pole or poles
bukpam baikait (n) arrogance
bukpiya (n) the condition of being an orphan
bukpokpo (n) nails (metal pieces)
bukpoorka (n) brownish teeth due to prolonged coating from food particles and lack of dental care
bukporkor (n) weakness, lacking the strength to fight
bukporor (n) harloting, promiscuity
bukuwi (n) shortness
bukuwiri (n) hairs
bukwa (n) impotence

bukwak (n) star fish
bukwa baikait (n) surprise; astonishment; a shock
bukwe (n) leopards; different branhes of the highest traditional society
e.g. 1. Bukwe bu de urum quu? *Are there leopards in this forest?*
2. O dion bukwe kpat bu chun. *He has been initiated into very branch of Ewke.*
bukwem (n) fish, fishes
bukwai (n) thorns; branches of fallen tree
bukwom (n) infertility, barreness
bukwop (n) scales
bumaat (n) scars
buman (n) birth (by a woman)
bumanko (n) mango trees
bumbe (pro) their, theirs (plural pronoun for singular or plural possessions)
e.g. 1. Biain bumbe ndior. *That is their thing.*
2. Bukam bumbe ndai. *These are their plantains.*
bumbet (n) policies; regulations; laws, bylaws; rules

Bumbet ba Orbasi (n) The commandments of God
bumboon (pro) your, yours (in plural, when "biain" is the signal word)
bumbume (n) questions
e.g. Buu aye bumbune. *Ask him/her questions.*
bumbuni (n) lame people; the lame
bumkpontong (n) throats
bumkpork (n) lizards
bumkpuk (adj) blind
e.g. N taaree bunkpuk. *I was blind.*
(adv) blindly
e.g. U noormi u sai biain bunkpuk. *It is not good to do things blindly.*
(n) blindness
e.g. Bunkpuk bu noormi. *Blindness is not good.*
bumkpuk bumkpuk (adv) blindly
bumi (pro) my, mine (for singular or plural possession)
e.g. 1. Biain bumi ndai. *This is my thing.*
2. Buria bumi ndior. *Those are my yams.*
bumork (n) an illness, illnesses; a sickness, sicknesses

bumorng (pro) his, her, it; his, hers, its (for plural possesion)
e.g. Bukam bumorng ndior. *Those are his/her plantains.*
bumooto (n) motors, vehicles, cars, lorries
bunaami (n) sheep
bunaang (n) fufu
buna ba dukpewi (n) subjects; branches of learning
e.g. 1. A kpewiri mmung buna ba dukpewi a enor a nkwet? *Which subjects are you studying in school?*
2. Nkwet e chorm ekese a buna ba dukpewi. *Education has branches of learning.*
bunanau (n) craw-craw
bunang ukwak (n) bicycles
bunchokoro (adj) naked; red handed
e.g. N kuba aye bunchokoro. *I caught him/her red handed.*
bunchori (n) a game played, with fruits in lieu of balls, like ping-pong
buneke esin (n) joy, joyousness; cheerfulness; happiness, jubilation; delight

buneke ingwa (n) sweet-tongue; flattery
bung (v) drive; paddle; pilot
e.g. A keme u bung mooto? *Can you drive a car?*
bungha (v) driving, drove; paddling, paddled; piloting, piloted
e.g. Meng o bungha uwan quor? *Who is paddling that canoe?*
bunghene (v) drive; paddle; pilot (done often)
e.g. M bunghene uwan umi kpokpora okum. *I paddle my canoe every week.*
bunghini (v) rub; caress
bungo (pro) your, yours (singular pronoun, for singular or plural possesion)
e.g. 1. Biain bungo ndai? *Is this your thing?*
2. Buka bungo ndai? *Is this your art work?*
3. Butoma bungo ndai. *These are your containers.*
bungyenghe ingwha (n) (lit.: sweet mouth) sweet-tongue; flattery
buninghene (n) familiarity; acquaintance

bunkarinka (n) bells; clocks
bunkarika ba ubor (n) wrist watches
bunkon (n) owls; mud fish (plurals of)
bunkoorn (n) joints
bunkpaka (n) buttons
bunkpanyan (n) rings
bunndiise(n) shows; spectacles; displays; exhibitions
bunning baikait (n) pride
bunoork (n) a bush cats
bunoorm (n) goodness
e.g. Ini u taina bunorm bubon ndai asik. *This is not the time to demonstrate our goodness.*
(adj) beautiful; good
e.g. Kwen bunorm! *What a beautiful child!*
bunoorm emaana (n) good manners, good behaviour
bunorm esin (n) good-heartedness; kindness
bunoorm kiro (n) good behaviour
bunoornga (n) beds; sex
bunoort (n) nails (of fingers or toes)
bonornghi (n) maggots
bunork (n) fights; wars
bunkwet (n) books; letters

bunkwet ba dono (n) (lit.: books of the head) identity cards; passports
bunsuk ikang (n) ships
buntak (n) insects
buntonini (n) worms
bunu (n) snakes
bunum (n) old age
bunumwok (n) red colobus monkeys
bunning baikait (n) pride
buntonini (n) worms
bunuum (n) millipedes
bunwam baikait (n) pride
bunyang (n) fartings
bunyenghe (adj) sweet
e.g. Orkem, bunyenghe! *Palm wine, so sweet!*
(n) sweetness
e.g. Kpara a taba bunyenghe ba orkem quor. *Don't follow the sweetness of that palm wine.*
bunyenyenghe (n) Indian bamboos
bunyi (n) elephants
bunyi ba mini (n) (lit.: water elephants) hippopotamuses
bunoom (n) red duikers
bunyorni (n) saliva (plural); spitting frequently (to have the habit of)
e.g. A ya kpai bunyorni. *You have the habit of spitting frequently.*

(adj) slippery slipperiness
e.g. Ainain, bunyorni! *The road, so slippery!*
buquai (v) [lit.: "Have you come?"] welcome (for two or more visitors)
buqun (n) belly; belly-ache; pregnancy
buququni (n) intestines
buquook (n) hip
bura (v) mean, means
e.g. Din dingo di bura ning? *What does your name mean?*
burang (n) lice
e.g. A chorm burang? *Do you have lice?*
bure (inf. v) are
e.g. words that begin with "bu" (including "bian") medicine go with "bure"
bureke (n) dirtiness; filthiness
buria (n) yams
buriem (n) fear, fright, apprehension
e.g. N chormi buriem nke kwanaka. *I don't have fear even one bit.*
bu rik (v) [lit.:"Have you returned?"] welcome (for two or more residents)
buron nen (n) the habit of frightening people into accepting deals against their will; bullying; intimidation
e.g. A ya buron nen. *You are fond of intimidation.*
buroror (n) [see also budordor] knowledge, understanding; cleverness; intelligence; shrewdness; wisdom
burou (adj) heavy (n) heaviness
buru esin (n) anger; annoyance
buruk (adj) another, other (for nouns beginning with "bu")
e.g. Baquai buria buruk. *Bring another yams.*
buruki (n) livestock, domestic animals
busa (n) witchcraft; sorcery
busak (n) rattles (musical instruments)
busaiki (adj) so bitter
e.g. Erop, busaiki. *Soup, so bitter!*
(n) bitterness
busokoro (n) oranges
busooja (n) soldiers
busorwa (n) chairs; seats, sofas; sittings, meetings
busorwa ba duborn (n) thrones
but (v) leave, get out

e.g. But ma. *Leave here / Get out of here.*
butaina baikait (n) showiness; ostentation
e.g. Butaina baikait bu noormi. *Ostentation is not good.*
buteemini (n) floor
e.g. Saa a butemini. *Sit on the floor.*
butort esin (n) ill temper; bad temper
e.g. Onerom quor or chorm butort esin. *That man has a bad temper.*
butort inghwa (n) great ability to convince by telling lies
but usene (v) [figurative] stand out, become distinguished; become successful in life, prosper
e.g. Kwen quor or ka but usene. *That child will become successful in life.*
buu (v) ask especially once
e.g. Buu aye. *Ask him/her.*
buubon (n) goats
buu daban (v) ask a hand in marriage
e.g. O buu mmi daban. *He has asked my hand in marriage.*
buuka (n) craftsmanship; an art; a work of art
buukoorn (n) hornbills

buukpaan (n) selfishness
e.g. Buukpaan bungo bu kpai nkang. *Your selfishness is beyond compare.*
buum (v) search for; scavenge, forage
Buumbet ba Orbasi (n) Disciples of God
buumkpork (n) lizards
buun (n) tortoises
buun ba mini (n) turtles
buuna (n) branches; tributaries
e.g. 1. Nkwet e chorm ekese a buuna. *Learning has many branches.*
2. Orkpa quo or chorm ekese a buuna. *This river has many tributaries.*
buunaami (n) sheep
buunkpok (n) tadpoles
buunoork (n) bush babies
buunoort (n) nails (of the finger or toe)
buura (v) burst; explode
buut (v) shoot; shot
buuwoka (n) buffaloes
buuwon (n) the act of a man producing children; the act of fathering children
buuwoort (n) giant rats (rat moles)
buwa (n) short-snouted crocodiles

buwi (v) ask (repeatedly or from one person to another); cross-examine
e.g. Be tornghor u buuwi aye bumbume. *They have started asking him/her questions/ They have started cross-examining*
buwindo (n) windows
buworm (n) cows
buwot (n) the habit of visiting or hanging around for free food
buwuri (n) waterfalls
e.g. I chorm ikpor a buwuri a Kororp. *There are many big waterfalls in Kororp.*
buya (v) stir (briefly and fast); stir up
e.g. 1. Buya mmi erop chor. *Stir that soup for me.*
2. Kpara buya ukwen quor daing. *Don't stir up that problem again.*
bu yaini (v) [lit.: *have you (plu.) woken up?*] good morning
buyairi (n) writing
buyairi ba neke (n) literature
buyini (n) boils
buyiri (n) length; height

Chch

cha (adv) that
e.g. Eta chai cha N ning ndai? *Is this the clothes that I saw?*

chaai (v) tear; torn especially a paper or leaf; scratch; scratched
e.g. 1. Bek kwen ongo or be chai bunkwet bumi. *Tell your child not to tear my books.*
2. Ket aranga or chaai nne baikait kpekpe na anyiri a bunoort bumorng bor. *See how he/she has scratched my body all with those his/her long nails.*

chaam (n) a medium sized fish with a small mouth and something like craw-craw on the nose; hence the pidgin name of "craw-craw nose"

chaani (v) untie e.g. a person who has been bound up with ropes, or a bundle or a tied bag

chaang (v) urinate

chaap (n) animal; meat; convulsion

chaap a disaing (n) buttock

chaari (v) yawn (repeatedly)
e.g. Or tornghor u chaari; u keni ngha or kwaka u rat. *He is beginning to yawn; it seems he is about to sleep.*

chabi (v) split open; tear apart

chai (prep) this
e.g. A kwaka eta chai? *Are you looking for this clothes?*

chain (v) answer
e.g. Orbasi or chain akam omi. *God has answered my prayer.*

chaina (v) greet; salute; thank

chiani (n) one
e.g. Chaap chaini. *One animal.*

chaka (v) castrate; reduce the quantity of, subtract from
e.g. 1. Or kwaka u chaka ebia emorng. *He wants to castrate his dog.*
2. U kaini ngha be chaka borkor be. *It looks like this food has be reduced.*

chama (v) squeeze (once or briefly)

cham (v) squeeze (continuously)

chamana (n) cuddle, embrace

e.g. Quai I chamana. *Come and let us embrace.*
chana (inf.v) plan (especially to do something)
e.g. A chana u quai? *Did you plan to come?*
chang (v) give; dedicate
e.g. 1. Chang mmi. *Give me.*
2. Chang daikwai dai a akam. *Dedicate this day to prayers.*
chang ataip (v) exaggerate; overstate; overrate
chang…itaim (v) advise
e.g. U normi u chang ben baingo itaim. *It is good to advise your children.*
chang…korou (v) give weight to; (figuratively) add value to; give credibility to; validate authenticate
chang ubor (v) shake hands with
e.g. Chang mmi ubor. *Shake hands with me.*
chang…ududu (v) permit; authorise; empower
e.g. 1. Mmi N chang aye ududu. *I am the one that permited him/her.*
changhana (v) dry something
e.g. Changhana ita ingo a dukwaing. *Dry your clothes in the Sun.*
changhi (v) get dry; will not give
e.g. Ita nyor I tornghor u changhi. *Those clothes are beginning to get dry.*
(adj) dry
e.g. Ita imorng I na changhi. *His/her clothes are not yet dry.*
changhi changhi (adj) dry
e.g. Ikwang nyor I rere ning ndior i changhichanghi? *Why are the leaves appreaing so dry?*
chani (v) untie e.g. a bundle; open up e.g. a zipped or tied bag; unscrew; unveil, unfold e.g. a parcel
chap urum (n) a beast (derogatory)
chari (v) yawn; make a statement clear by bringing out the hidden parts
chau (adj) many; much
e.g. Bene, bu chau! *People, so many!*
chawa (v) for a child to feed on or suck the breast; to suck, for example an orange.

41

e.g. Ntcm omi quo or chawa mumbi kpat or tap niet dio. *This my friend sucked until he reached ten years.*

chawara (v) for a mother to breast-feed a child

e.g. Ekese a baton be na chawara ben bembe kpat be woora niet niwan. *Many mothers suckle their children until they approach two years.*

chaawi (adj) many; not many

e.g. 1. Bene be chaawi kpai enor chai. *There are too many people in this house.*

2. Ita imi I chaawi daing a orkebe omi. *My clothes are not many again in my box.*

(v) scratch (continuously, with the nails)

e.g. Kpara chaawi mmi. *Don't scratch me.*

chawi (v) scratch (momentarily, with the nails)

e.g. Kpara a chawi nne. *Don't scratch me.*

chaya (v) tear; tore, torn; stratch, scratched (momentarily)

e.g. 1. Or chaya kobobiri ka nkwet keni kport. *He tore one sheet of paper only.*

2. Anwha or chaya aye. *A cat has scratched him.*

chee (v) gossip, gossiped; backbite, backbit; backstab, backstabbed

e.g. Or ya u chee bene. *He/she likes to gossip people.*

cheek (v) get burnt; burnt

e.g. 1. A kwaka u cheek? *Do you want to get burnt?*

2. Karia kaimi ke cheek. *My yam has burnt.*

cheeke (v) burning

e.g. Ekpa engo e cheeke. *Your bag is burning.*

chek (v) slice (e.g. vegetable or onion); tap (e.g. felled palm tree to get palmwine)

e.g. 1. Mbork, chek mmi oyim orkat quor. *Please, slice that onion for me.*

2. Amene ongo o nyi de chek nekem? *Has your father gone to tap palm wine?*

chekere (v) burn (e.g something or someone or onself

cheri (v) singe, singed; burn, burnt (slightly,

especially meat, to remove hair)

chiai (inj) an expression of self assurance or self-invigorating
e.g. Chiai! Mmi? U ngwei aye? *Chai! Me? To run away from him?*

chik (v) saw
e.g. Chik kabababi kor. *Saw that plank.*

chim (v) make a noise; to bear fruits
e.g.1. Kpara chim. *Don't make a noise.*
2. Etighi chai etornghor u chim. *This pawpaw tree has started to bear.*

chima (v) for many people to shout or make a noise in unison
e.g. 1. Chima nor. *Shout, all of you.*
2. Ini a i wot a enor emorng, I chorm u chima. *When we are near his/her house, we have to shout in unison.*

chin (v) did...wear; wore
e.g. Chin ben bor ita. *Wear those children clothes.*

chiina (v) dress up, wear (especially a loin-cloth round the waist)
e.g. Chiina usobo aba quai. *Wear a loin-cloth before you come.*

chiinaa (v) forget, forgot, forgotten
e.g. A chiinaa daikwai da I nenene ma. *Have forgotten the day we met here.*

chiinaa bangha (v) forget about

chini (v) undress, to remove one's clothes (especially a loin-cloth)

chioop (n) a porcupine

chiori (v) debark

chiork (v) swim

choba (n) plant or put a juju in a place (especially to prevent theft or witchcraft)
e.g. O choba ekpang emorng. *He/she has planted a juju in his/her farm.*

choi (v) wash; sanctify; purify

choi kibaain (v) cleanse (as a kind of deliverance from especially a traditional curse or other related problem)
e.g. Onerom quo o choi aton ongo kibaain. *This is the man who cleansed your wife.*

chok (v) shout (repeatedly to prevent an unwanted action against oneself);

suck, eat (especially orange or sugar cane).

choki (v) unhinge; separate a part from its frame

e.g. 1. Kpara choki ne butan ba diat. *Don't unhinge my jawbones.*

2. A kwaka u choki itum nyor? *Do you want to unhinge that door?*

chooka (v) shout (briefly, especially to prevent an unwanted action action against oneself)

e.g. N ya u chook ormankor. *I like to eat sugar cane.*

choom (v) fry

e.g. Or ya u chom daria demorng. *She likes to fry her food.*

choon (v) kill

e.g. U noormi u choon orne. *It is not good to kill a person.*

choong (v) hem

e.g. A biri choong ekpa chai, e ka fara chain. *If you don't hem this bag, it will loosen soon.*

(n) a crocodile (the long-snouted type)

chooni (v) killing, killed

e.g. 1. A chooni mmung ndior? *What are you killing like that?*

2. Mmung chap a chooni? *Which animal have you killed?*

choop (n) skin, hide; weight (fig to be fat)

choorba (v) lounge, sit comfortably (especially a fat or royal person, in a nice or relatively nice seat); recline (in a seat due to tiredness or feeling of weakness)

choork (v) grind

e.g. Ornaton quo or dor u choork orworna. *This woman knows how to grind tobacco.*

choormi (v) breathe (continuously), breathing

e.g. Sa ma a choormi kwanaka. *Sit here and breathe for a while.*

choormini (v) breathing

e.g. Mmung a choormini nyi ndior? *Why are you breathing like that?*

choorn (v) smoke (e.g cigarette); drink (once or briefly)

e.g. U noormi u choorn sika. *It is not good to smoke cibarettes.*

chor (prep) that

e.g. Baquai chaap chor ma. *Bring that animal/meat here.*

chork (n) chalk
(v) smash, smashed; crush, crushed
e.g. Kpara chork usan quor. *Don't smash that plate.*

chorhi (v) sharpen (continuously especially sticks or bamboos), clean (especially chewing sticks); plane (especially wood)
e.g. 1. Mbork, nyangha mmi u chorhi bunyenyenghe bor. *Please, help me sharpen those bamboos.*
2. Ornaton or ya ngo or chorhi chang ngo ukork. *If a woman loves you she cleans a chewing stick for you.*

chorm (inf. v) have, own; share (especially boundary with); need to
e.g. 1. A chorm inaii a nkwet? *Do you have a pen?*
2. N chorm uben na aye. *I share boundary with him/her.*
3. N chorm u chooya M ba quai. *I need to bathe before I come.*

chorma (v) own, owned; have, had
e.g. U normi u chorma ekpang. *It is good to own a farm.*

chorma dara daini (v) (figuratively) agree; reach a consensus
e.g. 1. Nik i chorma dara daini. *Let us agree.*
2. I na chorma dara daini a ukwen quor. *We have not yet reached a consensus on that issue.*

chormi (v) don't have; breathe, breath in; take a deep breath, heave a sigh of relief
e.g. 1. N chormi ekpang ma. *I don't have a farm here.*
2. Chormi! *Breathe in!*
3. Or chormi a ntak a ben bemorng be num. *He/she heaves a sigh of relieve because his/her children are big now.*

chorn (v) sing
e.g. Or ror u chorn dortor dai. *He/she knows how to sing this song.*

chorngha (v) send or push (through a hole)
e.g. chorngha esang chor a doboki dor. *Push the pipe through the hole.*

chornghi (v) cough
e.g. A kwaka u hornghi korngha, kpiya ingwa

ingo na ubor. *If you want to cough, cover your mouth with the hand.*

chornghini (v) coughing; coughed

e.g. 1. Meng or chornghini nyindior? *Who is coughing like that?*

2. Meng or chornghini? *Who coughed?*

choorn (v) smoke; drink (especially soup)

e.g. Kwen, kpara choorn siika. *Child, don't smoke cigerettes.*

choorni (v) smoke; drink, especially soup (continuously)

e.g. 1. Or ya u chorni siika. *He/she like to smoke cigarette.*

2. Choorni nduk chor e torort. *Drink that soup hot.*

choorng (n) a large-mouth fish in Kororp river, about or a little more than the size of a goldden barb

chooya (v) bathe; bathing

e.g. Chooya a ba quai. *Bathe before you come.*

chornn (v) snore

e.g. U re nyi a ka chornn ndaikwai. *It seems like you will snore tonight.*

chort (v) establish (i.e. for a plant to grow roots); for fire to start burning well

e.g. 1. Kainaii kor ke chot. *The tree has established roots.*

2. Dioon du chort. *The fire has started burning well.*

chorya (v) sharpen (momrntarily, especially a stick or bamboo); clean (momrntarily, especially a chewing stick)

chou (v) dance

e.g A dor u chou? *Do you know how to dance?*

chowa (v) warm one's self (e.g. at a fire); bask (especially in the Sun); warming, basking

e.g. 1. N chowa dion. *I am warming myself at a fire.*

2. O chowa dukwaing. *He/she is basking in the Sun.*

chu (n) kernel

chu ikoon (n) [lit: a kernel of a scrotum] a testicle

chuka (v) shut, close quickly (e.g. one door); quickly deposit especially a collection of items or things such as fuelwood

e.g. 1. Chuka itum nyor. *Shut that door.*
2. Chuka nanan nor ma. *Deposit those stones here.*

chuki (v) open (quickly e.g. one door); quickly pick up or gather a collection of items or things (such as fuelwood)
e.g. 1. Chuki itum nyor. *Open that door.*
2. Chuki nanan nor. *Gather those stones.*

chun (adj) finished; through (i.e. finished doing something)
e.g. 1. Daria de chun. *Food is finished.*
2. Ta bu chun? *Are you already through?*
(v) fold, fold up; completed (e.g. a course of study)
e.g. 1. Chun uboong quor. *Fold that floor mat.*
2. Ta a chun nkwet engo? *Have you completed your education?*

chuna (v) finish, conclude, complete, finalise
e.g. 1. A chuna duwom dungo? *Have you finished your work?*
2. Chuna ukwen ungo. *Conclude your talk.*

chuna daban (v) terminate e.g. a marriage, divorce
e.g. A kwaka a ibon I chuna daban dai. *Do you want us to terminate this marriage? Do you want us to divorce?*

chunene (v) bend (especially a hand); fold (especially an umbrella or a pen knife)
e.g. 1. Chunene ubor ungo. *Bend your hand.*
2. Chunene ufaikaiyo quor a ba kom. *Fold that umbrella before you keep it away.*

chunn (n) an axe
e.g. 1. A dor u koi kainaii na chunn? *Do you know how to fell a tree with an axe?*
2. Chunn chai e dowi kpai. *This axe is too heavy.*

chu orkat (n) a coconut

chuop (n) skin, hide, leather
e.g. Oborn a Ekorn or chorm chuop ekwe enor emorng. *The king of Ekon has a leopard skin.*

chuu (v) steal
e.g. A chuu a ba mana? *Have you stolen since you were born.*

chuuk (v) shut, close (e.g. many doors); place, pack a collection of items (e.g. fuelwood) orderly
e.g. 1. Chuuk muntum mor. *Shut those doors.*
2. Chuuk imet nyor ma. *Pack the fire wood here.*
chuuka (v) gather, assemble, congregate (especially many people)
e.g. 1. Chuuka nor ma. *Gather you here.*
2. Kwanaka bene be ka chuuka ma. *Soon people will gather here.*
chuuka a bukei (v) settle down
chuuki (v) open (e.g. many doors); pick up or gather a collection of items
e.g. 1. Chuuki muntum mor. *Open those doors.*
2. Chuuki imet nyor. *Collect the fire wood.*
chuum (n) an oracle of two strings made of bush mango shells
chuun (adj) be full, eaten to one's fill
e.g. N chuun. *I am full or I have eaten to my fill.*
chuuni (n) kidney
chuwa (adj) full

e.g. 1. Ekpa chor e chuwa. *That bag is full*
(v) to overflow its banks (especially a river)
e.g. 1. Orkpa o chuwa. *The river is full/ has overflown its banks.*
chuwere (v) fill; complete the amount or quantity of
e.g. 1. Chuwere kotom ke mi. *Fill my container.*
2. Chuwere munei mor *Complete that amount of money.*

Dd

da (pro) whose
e.g. Dorkorng da meng ndai? *Whose pot is this?*
daak (n) stammering
e.g. U korni u neme na orne or morka daak. *It is diffucult to discuss with someone who is suffering from stammering.*
daami (v) jump (continuously); hop
e.g. 1. Tornghor u daami. *Start to jump.*
2. Nansang ne tornghor u daami. *The frogs have started to hop.*
daamini (v) jumping; hopping
1. Ben bor be daamini mmang? *Where are those children jumping?*
2. N ya u ning arangha nansang ne daamini. *I like to se how frogs are jumping.*
daan (v) burst; rupture (especialy the eye)
e.g. A kwaka u daan aye den? *Do you want to burst his/her eye?*
daara (n) a tongue; a dilect
e.g.1. Choi daara gaingo ini ini. *Wash your tongue from time to time.*
2. Or tangha daara dairuk. *He/she speaks a another dilect.*
daat (v) [see also raat] sleep
e.g. N ka daat. *I will sleep.*
dabai (n) a breast
daban (n) marriage
dabana (n) sex
dabia (n) groin
dai (v) lick
e.g. N ya u dai munei mundooni. *I like to lick red palm oil.*
(adj) this
e.g. A kwaka dorkorng dai? *Are you looking for this pot?*
daibaing (adj short; half
e.g. 1. Daibaing da kainaii. *A short stick.*
2. Munok mundai munde daibaing ekpaime. *This drink is half in the bottle.*
(n) a half
e.g. A ka yau u deu daibaing? *Will you like to buy a half?*
daibin (n) a totem (in witchcraft); totemism
daichiina (n) fortgetfulness
daikait (n) a deep point in a river
daikwai (adv, n) day, daytime; weather

e.g. A daikwai a daikwai, bu chorm u nyi de chang Omuna uchaina a enor Orbasi. *Day by day, you have to go and give thanks to the Lord in church.*

daikwain (n) a scoop net for fishing

daing (conj) also, too; again

e.g.1. Chang mmi daing. *Give me also.*
2. A ya aye daing? *Do you love him/her also?*
3. U reni kwa a keme u sai daing. *There is nothing that you can do again.*
4. A dorni mmi daing? *Don't you know me again?*
5. Mbiri kwaka u ning ngo ma daing. *I don't want to see you here again.*

daingo (pro) your, yours (for singular possesion)
e.g. Taina mmi den daingo. *Show me your eye.*

daingdaikwai (adv) the day after tomorrow, the day before yesterday
e.g. 1. N dioni ma daindaikwai. *I arrived here the day before yesterday.*
2. N ka quai ndor daingdaikwai. *I shall come there the day after tomorrow.*

daini (n) one
e.g. Dobo daini. *One kolanut.*

dairuk (adj) another
e.g. N ning doboki dairuk. *I have seen another head.*

daisin (n) refusal; the habit of refusing especially to receive a gift

daisip (n) a calabash

daiyain (n) hatred
e.g. Daiyain de noormi. *Hatred is not good.*

dama (v) [see also rama] jump (once or briefly)
e.g. A ka keme u dama yeu ukani quor? *Will you be able to jump over that log of wood?*

dang (n) bladder

dang da mianghi (n) urinary bladder

dangwha [Duk.] (n) a door; doorway; (figuratively) pathway
e.g. Chuka dangwha dor. *Shut that door.*

dankanankan (n) three days ago; in three days time
e.g. 1. N dika quai dankanankan. *I returned three days ago.*

2. N ka dika quai dankanankan. *I shall return in three days time.*
danwha [Duk.] (n) a door
dara (v) [see also rara] rejoice, jubilate, celebrate
e.g. Nik I dara nor. *Let us rejoice.*
daria (n) food
dai (v) lick continuously; licking, licked
e.g. Kwen kwo or ya u dai usan na daara. *This child is fond of licking the plate with the tongue.*
daya (v) lick (momentarily)
dayawa (n) love
e.g. Nik I taina bantem dayawa. *Let us show others love.*
de (inf.v) [see also re] be; am; is; are
e.g. 1. Or de eti orne. *He/she is a good person.*
2. A de. [lit.: *Are you there?]* Good afternoon/Good evening.
dee (v) is not; has not; will not
e.g. 1. Dono da ukwen dee reni? *There is no headline?*
2. Donuna daimi dee na dion. *My luggage has not arrived.*

3. Donuna daingo dee ri dion ndaiquai. *Your luggage will not arrive today.*
deek (v) [see also reek] rest, relax; hold on
e.g. 1. Sa deek uka. *Sit and relax for a moment.*
2. Deek uka. *Hold on a moment.*
deekweem (n) light, enlightenment
e.g. 1. I totnghor u ning deekweem da Orbasi. *We have started to see the light of God.*
2. Ini a deekweem ndai. *This is the age of enlightenment.*
deemi (v) [see also reemi] whisper
e.g. Quai I deemi kwanaka. *Come and let us whisper a little.*
deemini (v) [see also reemini] whispering
e.g. A deemini mmung? *What are you whispering?*
deeni (v) is not, is no; are not, are no; is not available; not present, absent; is nothing; is no bad news
e.g. 1. Kwen ormorng or deeni a enor. *His/her child is not in the house.*

2. Bene be deeni ma. *There are no people here.*
3. Or deeni ndaikwai. *He/she is not present today.*
4. Biain bu deeni a enor. *There is nothing in the house.*
5. Kpara babi esin, biain bu deeni. *Don't panic, there is no bad news.*

deeyeeng (n) a find; a breakthrough, a discovery, an invention; act of finding something
e.g. Mmung u de orkporsonrg a deeyeeng a kaibain? *What is the greates discovery in the world?*

deeyeen (n) a plum

deeyeen da orkat (n) pear, alvocado

deke (v) [see also reke] dirty, make dirty or filthy
e.g. Kpara deke ita nyor. *Don't dirty those clothes.*
(adj) dirty, filthy
e.g. 1. Ita imi i deke kpai. *My clothes are too dirty.*
2. Eyain chai e deke kpai. *This place is too filthy.*

dei (n) night, night time
e.g. O rika na dei. *He returned in the night.*
(adj) night
e.g. N yani duseeng da dei. *I don't like night travel.*

dei dei (adv) by night
e.g. Or na dioni ma dei dei. *He often arrives here by night.*

dembe (pro) their; theirs (for singular possesion)
e.g. 1. Daban dembe de normi. *Their marriage is good.*
2. Daban dembe de fikiri norm. *Their marriage is not very good.*

dembinambin (n) a shade (protection from the Sun)
e.g. Nkui e yani dembinambin. *Maize does not like shade.*

demorng (pro) his/her/it; his/hers/its (for singular possesion)
e.g. Deeyeen demorng de bin. *His/her plum is black*

deen (n) eye
e.g. Tum kpii den daingo ko N quuna tor dumbio dor. *Open your eye well so I can blow off the speck.*

de na buqun (adj) with pregnancy
e.g. Or de na buqun. *She is with pregnancy.*

dendek (n) a hicup [Lit.: Hicup has caught me]

e.g. Dendek de kuba mmi. *I have a hicup.*
denen (n) a tooth
deng (v) sink
e.g. Erequa a morni kainaii kor a mini ke ka deng. *If you throw that stick into the water it will sink.*
dengdeng (n) pancreas
dere (inf. v) are (especially for words that begin with "da", "de" and "do" go with "dere")
e.g. Dobo dere ngo enor? *Is there a kolanut in your house?*
deruk (adj) another (for nouns beginning with "de", "dor", "do" or "da"
e.g. 1. Desip deruk ndai. *This is another calabash.*
2. N chorm dorkorng deruk. *I have another pot.*
3. N ning doboki deruk. *I have seen another hole.*
4. Be numa nne daria deruk. *They have brought me another food.*
desi (n) rice
e.g. N yani u dia desi a kporkporor ini. *I don't like to eat frequently.*
desor (n) a razor
e.g. Kpara ba desor daini a kporkpora bene. *Don't use one razor on everybody.*
deu (v) buy
e.g. N ka deu ekpa. *I shall buy a bag.*
di (adv) [see also ri] will not, won't; will never
e.g. 1. N di quai ma nyenene. *I will not come here again.*
2. N di chiina kwa a sai mmi. *I will never forget what you did to me.*
dia (v) eat; share especially boundary with; swear juju against oneself
e.g. 1. Ta a dia biain? *Have you eaten someting yet?*
2. N dia uben na aye. *I share a boundary with him/her.*
3. A keme u dia irot a ukwen quu? *Can you swear juju on this issue?*
dia ini (v) take a while, take some time
e.g. U ka dia ini M ba quai ma nyenene. *It shall take a while before I come here again.*
diaat (n) chin
dia inwha (v) boast; taunt (especially in order to overwhelm an oponent or ponents)

e.g. Or ya u dia inwha. *He/she is fond og boasting.*
dia isop (v) fine
e.g. Kpara a dia aye isop, or chormi munaii. *Don't fine him/her, he/she has no money.*
diana (v) add; include; attach
e.g. 1. N ka diana mumkpakot ita nyor M ba chang aye. *I shall add shoes to the clothes before I give to him/her.*
2. Diana aye a ndorng chai. *Include him/her in this team.*
dia unwornghor (v) swear; take an oath
e.g. Meng or keme u dia unwornghor a dono demorng. *Who can take a oath on him/her.*
dikere (v) put into an opening; insert, slot in
e.g. Dikere esang chor a doboki dai. *Insert that pipe into this hole.*
dien (adj, n) childish, childishness
Diet (n) Christmas
e.g. N ka re a dusai a Diet du. *I shall be in the village this Christmas.*
diet (n) year

c.g. N ka tornghor ikpor a dokoon a diet du. *I shall start a big farm this year.*
diimi (v) dive, swim (deep inside water)
e.g. Nik I diimi ma, ncheneruk I ka ning usan quor. *Let us dive here, we might find the plate.*
diin (n) a name
e.g. Din da meng ndai? *Whose name is this?*
diika (v) peep, peeped; peep into, peeped into
e.g. 1. Tum diika a ba kpaira utung na dei. *Peep well before you step out in the night.*
2. Meng or chang ngo ududu a diika a ubet umi? *Who gave you the audacity to peep into my bedroom?*
diikere (v) [see also riikere] peeping; peeping into
e.g. A dikere mmung? *What are you peeing?*
diim (adj) lost; extinct
e.g. 1. Ekpa emorng e diim. *His/her bag is lost.*
2. Bunyi bu diim katana kai. *Elephants are extinct in this area.*

dik (v) [see also dik] tinkle (someone repeatedly); return
e.g. 1. Kpara dik mmi. *Don't tinkle me.*
2. N ka fara dik. *I shall return soon.*

dika (v) [see also rika] tinkle (someone briefly); returned
e.g. 1. Meng or dika mmi? *Who tinkled me?*
2. N dika ndaikwai. *I returned today.*

dik quai (v) [see also rik quai] return
e.g. Dik quai enor aranghaquo. *Return home now.*

dim (v) go under water, dive, submerge

dima (v) [see also rima] misplace (something); put out (fire or light); destroy; cause to become extinct, exterminate, decimate
e.g. 1. A dima inaii a nkwet ingo? *Have you misplaced your pen?*
2. Kpara a dima ichap urum ubon. *Do not exterminate animals in our forest.*
3. Bunork bu keme u dima isai. *Wars can decimate villages/towns/cities.*

dimi (inf. v) stop; desist from; allow
e.g. Dimi ndior. *Stop like that.*
2. Dimi keche. *Desist from gossiping.*
3. Dimi (mmorng) o kaik. *Allow him/her to go.*

dingo (pro) your; yours
e.g. Din dingo ndai? *Is this your name?*

dioka (n) tree felling
e.g. I chun dusei, aranghaquo I chum u tornghor dioka. *We have finished clearing, now we should start tree felling.*

diomi (adj) small (always precided by any noun or pronoun)
e.g. Chap chai e diomi kpai. *This animal is too small.*

dion (v) enter, get into; arrive, arrived; get initiated into
e.g. 1. Dion enor. *Get into the house.*
2. Ta be dion? *Have they arrived?*
3. O dion Ekwe. *He has been initiated into Ekwe.*
(n) light; fire; gun
e.g. 1. Dion du reni a enor chai? *Is there no light in this house?*

2. Seng de kpoork dion a enor ekup. *Go and make a fire in the kitchen.*
3. A biri de ata atutaip erequa a chormi dion. *You are not a real hunter if you don't have a gun.*

dion quai (v) enter
diork [Duk.] (n) swimming
diort (n) trunk (especially of an elephant)
disaing (n) anus; buttocks
disaing da kainaii (n) foot of a tree
Disemba [from Eng.] (n) December
diyain (adv) tomorrow; yesterday
diyainikwai (adv) tomorrow; yesterday
dobo (n) a kolanut
dobok (n) a small bundle (e.g. of cooked food)
doboki (n) a hole
doboki da ufort (n) pith
doboki da disaing (n) anus
doboki da ichon (n) nostril
doka (v) [see also roka] do a piece of work in instalments; pay a debt or a fee in installments
e.g. N ka doka kpe maruum mengo. *I will pay an installment of your debt.*
doki (v) [see also roki] scrape off or remove quickly from a hole; scoop out from a shell
dokon (n) farm
dokui (n) an electric fish
dokum (adj) a desire to eat meat
dormbou (adj) left hand; left side
domuuk (n) the act of putting too much food into the mouth at a time before chewing, devouring
don (v) become red; become ripe
e.g. 1. Nen naingo ne ka don erequa a biri que de kpe maruum maingo. *Your eyes will become red if you don't come and pay your debt.*
donene nen (v) [see also ronene nen] intimidate, intimidating
e.g. 1. Kpara a donene ibon nen. *Don't intimidate us.*
2. Or ya u donene bene nen. *He/she fond of intimidating people.*
dono (n) head; headache; (figuratively) wisdom

e.g. 1. Kpara a tunghene dono daingo a windo a moto. *Don't send out your head through a car window.*
2. Or morka dono. *He/she is sick of headache.*
3. Kwen omi orchorm dono. *My child has some wisdom.*

dono dukwen (n) headlines; salient points; purpose

doona (n) a traditional stove made usually of three stones on which a pot is placed and between which fuelwood is stocked

donuna (n) luggage, baggage; freight; load, burden

dong (v) bite (once or briefly)
e.g. Erequa a korbor obaii a durum na ebia, e ka dong ngo. *If you are fond of rough games with a dog, it will bite you.*

dongha (v) does…bite or do…bite
e.g. Ebia chai e dongha seeng? *Does this dog sometimes bite?*

donghi (v) bite (continuously, a group, or in a group)
e.g. Bubia bu bu ka bonghi mbon. *These dogs will bite you.*

donghini (v) biting
e.g. Bini bi donghini mbe. *Ants are biting them.*

dooki (v) [see also rooki] scrape off or remove (from a shell)
e.g. Nik N dooki osorsoi. *Let me remove snails from the shells.*

dookiri (v) scraping off or removing (from a shell)

dookon (n) a farm
e.g. N chorm ikpor a dookon. *I have a large farm.*

dookuut (n) canopy (of a forest)
e.g. Ikpesinghi I re a urum a ntak a dookuut. *There is darkness in the forest because of the canopy.*

doong (n) a bundle, a parcel
e.g. 1. A baquai doong de mi? *Have you brought my parcel?*
2. Meng or chorm doong da imet dai? *Who has this bundle of fire wood?*

doop (n) navel
e.g. Kwen quo or chorm anorm a doop. *This child has a beautiful navel.*

doork (v) use invectives or abusive language on someone, rain abuses on someone or people
e.g.1. Doork na aye. *Use abusive language on him/her.*
2. Doork na aye. *Rain abuses on him/her.*
doorkin (n) lock
doorn (v) make a hole through; burst
doornor (n) a finger; a toe
dooroong (n) propensity to bite
e.g. Kwen quor or ya dooroong. *That child has the propensity to bite.*
doowom (n) a large wild fruits used for poisoning fish.
dor (v) [see also ror] know; understand, comprehend; master
e.g. 1. N dor din dimorng. *I know his/her name.*
2. N dor qua or tangha bangha. *I know what he/she is talking about.*
3. Or nekeri dor dubung. *He/she has not really mastered driving.*
dorbork (n) behind, backwardness; rear
e.g. 1. Be taak borbork. *They have remained behind.*
2. Dorbork de noormi. *Backwardness is not good.*
(adj) backward
e.g. Kororp ke biri de dorbork a kporpora a biain. *Kororp is not backward in everything.*
dorbork dorbork (adv) backward
e.g. Ini a or taba aiyain chai, or tornhor u seng dorbork dorbork. *When he/she got to this point, he/she started walking backward.*
dorbort da urung (n) morter pestle
dor buuka (adj) talented; gifted
e.g. Kwen quo or dor buuka. *This child is talented.*
dork (v) pound (especially palmnuts); boil; babble
e.g. 1. Tum dork nerei nor. *Pound those palm nuts well.*
2. Nik mini mor mu tum dork. *Let the water boil well.*
3. Kwen quo or tornghor u dork ukwen. *This child has started to babble a language.*
dorkorng (n) pot
dorktor [from Eng.] (n) doctor
dormbou (n) left hand

(adj) left side
dormorn (v) a voice; a statement; an opinion
dorni (v) don't know; don't understand
e.g. Bai dorni kwa kwen quor or keme u sai. *They don't know what that child is capable of doing.*
dornyorm (n) a mango (fruit, the wild type)
dorom (n) a knee
dobo (n) a kola nut
dorng (n) a trousers
dornor (n) a toe; a finger
doronghi (n) backyard (behind or rear part of a house); (figuratively) toilet; (figuratively) bathroom, mensroom or ladies room, to excrete or urinate
e.g. 1. Doronghi daimi de kanghi. *My backyard is large.*
2. Mbork, de taina mmi doronghi. *Please, show me to the toilet*
4. N ka nyi doronghi. *I will go to the bathroom.*
(adj) [lit.: in the backyard] (also figuratively) nearby
e.g A keri a kitum kor ki re ma doronghi? *You thought that the hut was just nearby? (*
dortor (n) a song
dortorp (n) mud (singular)
dorya (n) lawyer
dotuma (n) a pillar
dotutui (n) a person used to one's advantage, especially to experiment one's ability or strength; the marginalized
e.g. be re atata dotutui. *They are the most marginalized.*
drorm (n) [from Eng.] drum (container)
du (v) is, is not; will, will not (only accent changes the meaning)
e.g. Orkporsonrg a durum du noormi. *Too much playing is not good.*
duba (v) hide (someone or something)
e.g. Ni i duba mundiai mubon ma. *Let us hide out cutlasses here.*
dubaima (n) acceptance; consent
dubam (n) side
e.g. Or sou a dubam dumi. *He/she is sitting by my side.*
dubam da orkpa (n) a river bank
dubanana (n) a banana (fruit)

dubebiri (n) flying
dubeng (n) bundle (especially of thatches); a traditional cage for carrying especially life chicken; (figuratively) a burden
dubi (v) take or come out of a hiding place
dubiabiri da bukei (n) soil impoverishment
dubinini (n) sighing
e.g. Or ya dubinini. *He/she is fond of sighing.*
Dubiobio (n) Ibibio language
Duboong (n) Aboong variant of Durorp
dubor (n) a sheath, a scabbard
duborn (n) kindship; tenure of office as king
dubou da bukei (n) land degradation
dubowa (n) waste (of something)
dubung (n) driving; paddling
e.g. Or na tum dor dubung. *He/she has not mastered driving well.*
dubunghini (n) caressing
e.g. Or ya bubinghi. *He/she like caressing.*
dubut (n) wall

duchamana (n) an embrace; the act of cuddling or embracing
duchana (n) a plan, a programme, an arrangement
e.g. A chorm duchanai? *Do you have a plan /programme/arrangement?*
duchanghani (n) drying, smoking (of something such as fish)
duchanghini (n) drying up (especially of a stream or wet clothes)
duchai (n) a stream
duchiork (n) swimming
e.g. N ya duchiork. *I love swimming.*
duchoka (n))shouting (the act of)
duchokari (n))a shout
e.g. Duchokari duni ndornandor a tornghor u tikiri? *Only one shout and you start trembling?*
duchom (adj) fried
duchoorn (adv) gradually, gently, slowly; carefully, diligently
e.g. 1. Seng duchoorn a aiyain chai. *Move gently in this place.*
2. Sai duwom duchoorn. *Work diligently.*
3. Seng duchoorn. *Go well.*

duchorkiri (n) the act of destroying
duchorkiri da urum (n) deforestaion
e.g. Duchorkiri da urum du biri de aiti a biain. *Deforestation is not a good thing.*
duchorma (n) wealth; riches
duchukari (n) shutting (e.g. of the door)
duchunini da borkor ba urum (n) species extinxtion
dudap da nen (n) an eye lash
duduba (n) hidden, secret
du esin (v) be angry, be annoyed
e.g. Mbork, kpara du esin. *Please, don't be angry/annoyed.*
(adj) angry, annoyed
e.g. A du esin? *Are you angry/annoyed?*
dufaam (n) a boast; a taunt
dufaamini (n) boasting; taunting
e.g. A rere a onum emana engo chai a dufaamini? *Your are still in this your old habit of boasting?*
dufore (n) prosperity
Dufrench (n) French language

dufufuk (n) a midge
e.g. Nke dufufuk a ninghi ma a ntak a bioi. *You can't find even a midge here because of the cold.*
Dujaman (n) German language)
dukaap (n) taking sides (especially in a quarrel)
e.g. Dukaap du noormi. *Taking sides is not fair.*
dukain (n) a tail
dukakai (n) a thatch
dukakiri (n) crawling, creeping
dukam (n) a plantain (fruit)
dukan (n) a quarrel
Dukat (n) English language
duken (n) a state of being, or feeling like, a stranger or visitor
dukere (v) twist, sprain (especially the ankle or foot accidentally)
e.g. Kating a dukere uwon ungo? *Does it mean you have sprained your foot.*
duki (v) somersault (once or briefly); tumble; turn (especially clothes or a bag inside-out); prepare (especcially the limbs of a butchered animal for drying and sale by

stretching them out with sticks)
(adj) dangerous; cruel; malicious
e.g. O duki. *He/she is dangerous.*
dukoon (n) calling (the act of); reading (the act of); a reading or a passage
dukoork (n) crowing (the sound; the act of)
e.g. 1. A kpanghi dokoork dor? *Are you hearing that crowing?*
2. Kwen orom unorn quu ta or tornghor dukoork. *This cockerel has started crowing.*
Dukorn (n) Ekon variant of Durup
dukoko (n) a feather
dukona (n) a call; an invitation, invitation
e.g. N de ma a dukona dungo. *I am here on your invitation.*
dukoni (n) remembering
dukora (n) the phenomenon of being swept away by water
dukora da bukei (n) soil erosion
Dukoryorng (n) Orkoryorng variant of Duroorp
Dukpa (n) Ejagham language

dukpai (n) a kernel (especially of mango); a lip (especially of virgina)
dukpak (adj) poverty
e.g. Dukpak du noormi. *Poverty is not good.*
dukpain (n) colloquial or idiomatic language; history, a thing of the past
e.g. 1. Or dorni dukpain. *He/she does not understand colloquial language.*
2. Ekese kwa a tangha quor u ki de dukpain. *Much of what you say is now history.*
dukpaing (n) wriggling (usually in bed while in deep sleep)
e.g. 1. N yani u norngha na orne quo or ya dukpaing. *I don't' like to share a bed with someone who has the habit of wriggling.*
dukpangha (n) a bolt; a lock
e.g. Itum nyor i chormi dukpangha. *That door has no lock/bolt.*
dukpanghani (n) locking, bolting (e.g. of the door)

dukpanghini (n) hearing, feeling, tasting (the act of)

dukpari (n) road; highway
e.g. Dusai dubon du biri chormi dukpari. *Our villages did not have a road.*

dukpeem (n) begging (especially for something from someone)
e.g. Or ya kpai dukpeem. *He/she is too fond of begging.*

dukpekiri (n) limping

dukpewi (n) study, studies, research; internship, practice appentriceship, training
e.g. 1. N chang ekese a ini imi a dukpewi. *I dedicate most of my time to studies.*
2. O sai dukpewi da bangha ichap. *He/she is doing research on animals.*
3. Kwen omi or re a dukpewi. *My child in on intership.*

dukpewi da bainaii (n) botany
e.g. Nik ben bebon be sai dukpewi da bainaii. *Let our children do botany.*

dukpewi da dukuk da munaii (n) accountancy
e.g. Ben bebon be tornghor u sai dukpewi da munaii. *Our children have doing accountancy.*

dukpewi da ichap (n) a zoology; biology
e.g. I chaawi a dukpewi da ichap. *We are not many in zoology.*

dukpewi da kaibain (n) geography
e.g. e.g. Nik I tornghor u dion a dukpewi da kaibain. *Let start moving into Geography.*

dukpewi da bukemika (n) chemistry
e.g. Nik I tornghor u dion a dukpewi da bukemika. U normi u dion dain a dukpewi da kaibain. *It is good to move also into Chemistry.*

dukpewi da mbuk (n) journalism
e.g. Nik I bai chiina bangha dukpewi da mbuk. *Let us not forget about journalism.*

dukpewi da muntort (n) ornithology
e.g. Dukpewi da muntort du re daing eti a ekikere. *Ornithology is also a good idea.*

dukpewi da urum (n) forestry

e.g. Dukpewi da urum du ka re biain ba nfon. *Forestry will be an advantage.*

dukpewiri (n) learning, studies

e.g. Ben baimi be bowa ekese a ini imbe a dukpewiri, nkwor u sai be yewe nkwet embe. *My children spend much of their time in studies, which is the reason why they passed their exams.*

Dukpokobait (n) Okpokobait variant of Durup

dukpukiri (n) touch; touching (the act of)

e.g. A dukpukiri duni kport, or na buki buki. *With only one touch, he/she just woke up.*

dukpuukiri (n) touching (the act of)

dukuk (n) counting

e.g. Kating a dorni dukuk? *Does it mean you don't know counting?*

dukumanbiere (n) banana (native species harder than the common species); an indirect or euphemistic name for plantain

dukumini (n) the act of walking with pounding footsteps, especially as a show of pride or power

dukura (n) volition

e.g. M biri nyi a dukura dumi. *I did not go out of my own volition.*

Dukusa (n) Hausa language; an extra-large loin-cloth

dukwai (n) tenure as queen; a show of female pride

dukwaing (n) the Sun

e.g. Dukwaing di naimi. *The Sun is shining.*

dukwaing da kito (n) [lit.: the moring Sun] the rising Sun

dukwaing da kori (n) [lit.: the evening Sun] the setting Sun

dukwak (n) star fish

dukwor (n) death

e.g. Ta bu kpang dukwor da orborn? *Have you death about the death of the chief?*

dum (v) smel, give out a smell

e.g. Eyain chai etornghor u dum. *This place is beginning to smell.*

duma (v) rumble [also ruma] (e.g. for thunder or stomach to) e.g. Kwanaka buqun bumi bu ka duma. *Soon my stomach will rumble.*

dumbaap (n) plantain or banana harvested that is not mature enough to be harvested

dumbaap da banana (n) harvested banana that is not mature enough for harvesting

dumbaap da katam (n) harvested plantain that is not mature enough for harvesting

dumbaat (n) side pain, possibly inflammation of the spleen, as an illness in children

dumbio (n) a speck; a fault (figurative for)
e.g. 1. Dumbio du dion nne a den. *A speck has gotten into my eye.*
2. Or fara u ning dumbio a den da orne oruk. *He/she is fast to find a fault in someone else.*

dumeen (n) habitual drinking
e.g. Or ya kpai dumeen. *He/she is too fond of drinking.*

dumeke (n) familiarity; habituation

dumi (adj) smelly

e.g. Aiyain chai e dumi. *This place is smelly.*

dunkpa (n) a pincer (of a crab or prawn)

dunabiri (n) lack, scarcity (state of)

dunam (n) a penis

dunang (n) a bamboo (from oil palm or raffia palm)

dunchai (n) a prawn

dunchangha (n) a crayfish

dundoni (n) a ripe banana (especially)or plantain

duneiri (n) clearing
e.g. Aya duneiri bor dusorbiri? *Do you like clearing or weeding?*

Dunenghe (n) Ibo (language)

dung (v) live
e.g. A ka dung na mmi? *Will you live with me?*

dunghene (v) [see also runghene] investigate; inspect, examine; verify
e.g. 1. Be ka dunghene ngo a ukwen quu. *They will investigate you on this issue.*
2. Be na dunghene kwa a morka? *Have they not yet examined what you are sick of?*
3. Dunghene ukan quor a ba dor arangha a ka boror. *Verify the message*

before decide how to respond.

dunghi (v) [see also runghi] live, living
e.g. 1. N dunghi ma. *I live here/I am living here.*

dungo (pro) your, yours (in singular)
e.g. 1. Taina dunyor dungo ma. *Show your face here.*
2. Dunyor du du re dungo. *This face is your.*

duninghini (n) [lit.: seeing] recognition
e.g. U normi u taina aye duninghini a kwa or sai a dusai dubon. *It is good to show him/her a mark of reccognition for what he/she has done for our village.*

dunni da ekpaime (n) bottle-top

dunkon (n) mud fish

dunkpok (n) a large, single pronged metal gong; also used as an insult for a large nose
e.g. 1. Ket ichon ingo ngha dunkpok. *See your nose like a large metal gong.*

Dunkondokondo (n) Ikondokondo variant of Durorp

Dunkondup (n) Nkondup variant of Durorp

dunkui (n) a maize (cob or plant)

dunsoom (n) tissue; fibre

duntonini (n) a worm

dunukari (n) bending (the act of)
e.g. Dunukari du kpai aye. *Bending is above him/her.*

dunum (n) old-age, seniority, senility

dunun (n) a thorny, wild rope used especially for weaving traditional fishing cage-traps.

dunung (n) an ear

dunuwiri (n) a caterpillar (of an insect)
e.g. Duniwiri da ornkenenken ndai. *This is the carperpillar of a butterfly.*

dunwerp (n) digging, hoeing

dunwha (n) grave

dunwingnwing (n) a mosquito

dunwor (n) camwood powder
e.g. Baton ba Kororp bairuk be ya u korma dunwor. *Some Kororp women like to rub camwood powder.*

Dunyaang (n) Banyangi language

dunnyiort (n) a massage

e.g. Kpekpera koori o quai ma a dunnyiort. *Every evening he/she comes here for a massage.*

dunyor (n) face, front, in front, ahead

e.g. Choi dunyor dungo kito sik sik. *Wash your face early in the morning.*

duquang (n) a leaf

e.g. Kwaa mmi duquang dor. *Pick me that leaf.*

duququni (n) an intestine

durap da nen (n) an eye lid

durau (n) sleep; dream; vision

e.g. 1. Durau do nuu mmi. [lit.: *sleep is paining me*] *I am sleepy.*

2. N ning durau. [lit.: *I saw a dream*] *I had a dream.*

dure (inf. v) is, are; e.g. nouns that begin with "du" go with "dure"

Dure (n) Efik language, language of Calabar people

durek (n) a jaw

dureet (n) the habit of crying frequently (of a child)

burek (n) a jaw

durekeri (n) the act of making dirty

dubuiiri da mini (n) water pollution

duri (v) frown

durik (v) a rope

durion (n) arrival

e.g. Durion dubon ndai. *This is our arrival.*

durom (n) manhood

Durorp (n) the language of Kororp ethic group; Kororp language; language

duruba (adj) hiding

e.g. Or re re a duruba ta ne eye. *He/she is in hiding up until now.*

duruk (adj) another, other (for nouns that begin with "du"

e.g. 1. Duchai duruk du re tanana kor ndor. *Another stream is found that way.*

2. Duchai duruk du reni ma. *There is no other stream here.*

durup (n) secret, top-secret

e.g. Ukwen quu u biri de daing biain ba durup. *This issue is no longer a secret.*

durup durup (adv) secretly, clandestinely, surreptitiously, stealthily, sneakily

e.g. O dioni quai ma durup durup. *He/she entered here steathily.*

durum (n) play, entertainment; a joke
e.g. 1. Ini a durum ndai asik uka. *This is not play time yet.*
2. U re durum bor amang a ukwen? *It is a joke or a serious issue.*
durumani (n) smelling, sniffing (the act of)
durumini (n) smelling (the state of)
durut (n) eel, a long, thin fish that resembles a mud fish; commonly called snake fish
dusaang (n) disappearance
e.g. Dusaang da ebia chor du qua ibon baikait aiti aiti. *The disappearance of that dog has shocked us badly.*
dusai (n) village, town, city
Dusai da Ire (n) Calabar city
dusasam (n) running stomach, cholera; watery stool
e.g. 1. N chorm dusasam. *I have a running stomack.*
2. Kwen quo or nye dusasam. *This child is passing out watery stool.*
duseek (n) laughter, laugh

duseeng (n) walking, a walk; a travel, a journey; travelling; gait
e.g. 1. Kwen omi ta or tornghor duseeng. *My child has started walking.*
2. Amene omi o nyi duseeng. *My father has gone on a journey.*
3. Aminkei omi or ya duseeng. *My brother/sister likes travelling.*
4. N kaini amene omi a duseng. *I resemble my father in gait.*
dusei (n) clearing, slashing (the act of)
e.g. Be tornghor daing dusei a ekpang aimi. *They have also started clearing in my farm.*
duseiri (n) clearing, slashing (as a method)
e.g. Duseiri na dusorbiri, a ya nquni? *Slashing and weeding, which do you prefer?*
dusiin (n) a root
dusit (n) care-taking
dusorbari (n) boiling (as a method)
dusorbiri (n) weeding (as a method)
dusoorp (n) pushing
dusorsoi (n) a small snail that often destroys the

vegetative parts of crops
dusuwi (n) a vein
e.g. U korni u ning dusuwi da kwen or chorm orkporsorng a choop. *It is difficult to find the vein of a child who has a lot of weight.*
dut (v) rise (e.g. flour due to addition of water or something)
e.g. Erequa a tumi chooma kari ke keme u dut ini a norba nkor a mini. *If you fry gari well it can rise well when you soak it in water.*
dutang (n) rib, side
dutara (n) staggering
dutchoomini (n) frying
dutchori (n) a cane rope
dut duborn (v) feel proud like a king, for a man to show excessive pride
e.g. Kpara dut duborn dor na mmi. *Don't show such excessive pride towards me.*
dut dukwai (v) feel proud like a queen, for a woman to show excessive pride
dutaina (n) teaching; training; coaching
e.g. U kaini ngha or ya dutaina. *It seems like he/she likes teaching.*
dutoi (n) removal, unloading
dutoi da buqun (n) abortion
e.g. Dutoi da buqun du noormi. *Abortion is not good.*
dutoka (n) landing (the act of)
e.g. U korni u kuba itork ini a dubebiri kpai ini a dutoka. *It is not more difficult to catch a bird when it is flying than when it is landing.*
dutokiri (n) pinch, pinching (the act of)
dutort da kaibain (n) global warming
e.g. I tornghor u kpang dutort da kaibain. *We are beginning to experience global warming.*
duton (n) womanhood
dutonghantong (n) umbilical cord
dutornghor (n) start, beginning; commencement; introduction
e.g. Dutornghor da daria ndai. *This is just the beginning of the meal.*
dutuk (n) division, sharing; share; distribution, supply, allocation

e.g. 1. Ta be tornghor dutuk da munaii mor? *Have they started the sharing of that money?*
2. Ta a chorma dutuk dungo? *Have you had your own share?*
3. Ta be tornghor dutuk san an. *They have started the distribution of the medicines.*

dutuum (n) a walking stick

dutuuk (n) cheating

duuba (v) hide oneself or ourselves
e.g. Nik i duuba ma. *Let us hide here.*

duudiim (n) state of getting or becoming lost; extinction

duuki (v) somersault, tumble (continuosly); turn inside-out (especially clothes or a bag); prepare the limbs of a butchered animal for drying

duukuum (n) pounding foot steps
e.g. A kpanghi duukuum dor. *Are you hearing the pounding footsteps?*

duum (v) play, play (e.g. a musical instrument or set such as a guitar, a radio, a video player); joke
e.g. 1. Quai I duum. *Come and let's play.*
2. A dor u duum kita? *Do you know how to play the guitar?*
3. Kpara duum na mmi. *Don't play/joke with me.*

Dumm chang (v) entertain
e.g. Duum chang ibon. *Entertain us.*

duuma (v) smell; sniff; rumbling; playing, joking
e.g. 1. Duuma ekpaime chai. *Smell this bottle.*
2. Echong a duuma. *The sky is rumbling.*
3. Bu duuma na meng? *Who are you playing/joking with?*

duuma chang (v) entertaining
e.g. Be duuma chang ibon. *They are entertaining us.*

duumaan (n) a kick

duuni (n) a cork; one
e.g. 1. Duuni da ekpaime aimi ndai. *This is the cork of my bottle.*
2. N ka dia bukam duuni kport. *I will eat one plantain only.*

duunsaam (n) a big, long cage-trap made of cane

ropes used once in a long while for fishing, especially by a traditional society

duuruum (n) playing (especially of children) a play; a display; a concert; a performance; a show

duut (v) froth, foam
e.g. Orkem quo or tornghor u duut. *This palm wine has started to foam.*

duuwom (n) a wooden gong

duuwam (n) thunder
e.g. Duuwaam du chork kitum kimorng. *Thunder has destroyed his/her hut.*

duwaam (adj) half; piece; part
e.g.1. Duwaam da bene beyani. *Half of the people do not like/are not in support/favour.*
2. Duwaam da eta. *A piece of cloth.*
3. Chang mmi duwan da munaii mor. *Give me part of that money.*

duwewei (n) lightning
e.g. Duwewei du maya ko duuwaam du nor. *Lightning twinkles before thunder strikes.*

duwom (n) work; a duty; a function; a job, an occupation; a profession; a career; a vacancy, an opening

duwom da nookoon (n) farming

duwoorn (n) decay, decomposition; putrefaction

duwou (adj) roasted, burning

duwouwiri (n) roasting

duyebiri (n) stalking

duyei (n) shouting; barking; yelling (the act or habit of)

duyewiri (n) crossing point (especially on a river or stream); act of crossing

duyik (n) a horn

duyik da enyi (n) elephant trunk

duyik da orkat (n) (lit: a whiteman's horn) telephone; phone; mobile phone

duyik da mini (n) a rainbow

duyim (n) an onion

duyome (n) wandering, itinerant or nomadic lifestyle

duyoror (n) perambulation, strolling; strolling

display (especially of a masquerade)

duyorp (n) deception, deceit

Ee

e (inf.v) is, has
e.g. 1. Chap e quai.
An animal has come.
2. Chaap e re.
There is meat.
3. Eyain chai e noormi.
This place is not good.
4. Chaap chor e na qua.
That animal has not died yet.
5. Ebia chor e ri quai. *That dog will not come.*
ebam (n) a pocket
ebariba (n) a blacksmith
ebat (n) shoulder, hand of planatain or banana
ebep (n) a storm, windstorm
ebeng (n) the way; the manner in which
e.g. 1. Dor ebeng a seeng.
Know the way you move.
2. Ebeng a seeng dioni enor aimi, a sai a mi nchoma nsai eruk e bangha ngo. *The manner in which you walked into my house makes me have another opinion/idea about you.*
ebia (n) a dog
ebom (n) a fall

ebon (pro) our; ours (for singular or plural possesions)
e.g. 1. Ebia ebon ndai. *This is our dog.*
2. Efain ebon ndai. *These are our people.*
eebon (n) a goat
eenoork (n) a bush baby
echari (n) a bitter kola seed
echimini (n) fruit, fruits
e.g. I ka chorma echmini a diet du. *We shall have fruit this year.*
echong (adv) up
(n) the short form of "echong-adubut"
echong a yhion (n) uphill, mountaintop
e.g. Nya u baat echong a yhion. *I like to stand on the mountaintop.*
echong a dubut (n) sky
Echong Orbasi (n) Heaven
e.g. Meng or yani u yen Echong a Orbasi? *Who does not like to go to Heaven?*
echong ekai (n) roof
echong urum (n) canopy (forest)
echor (n) a snail, (figuratively) a slow or lazy person

echuwa (n) floods; problems (used figuratively for)

ediaimi (n) a plan (to do something); a plot; an agreement

ediki (adj) small; a little
  e.g. Chang mmi nyenene ediki. *Give me a little again.*

edidiki (adj) small
  e.g. Chaap edidiki. *Small animal/meat.*

edising (n) knife

eenhe (adj) yes

eenyaam (n) an eagle

eeru [Duk.] (n) vagina

eesaaing (n) an egg

efain (n) the people of; supporters; team members; acquaitances; relatives
  e.g. Efain a nasona pak be quai. *The National Park people have come.*

efain a duwom (n) workers
  e.g. Efain a duwom baimi ndai. *These are my workers.*

efain ita (n) [lit.: people of uniforms] law enforcement officers

Efaing (n) a Kororp festival that takes place after every seven years and lasts for a week in continuous celebrations marked by displays pf masquarades of various types

efore (n) ill-luck, misfortune

Epaire [from Eng.] (n) April

ekai (n) thatches

ekan (n) age grade; equal

ekanekan (adv) equally, the same, in the exact copy or state, exactly
  e.g. 1. Tuk borkor bor ekan ekan. *Share that food equally.*
  2. Or yiri ngha ngo ekan ekan. *He/she is [exactly] as tall as you.*

ekaang (n) fatness

ekeem (n) a bat
  e.g. Ekeem e ninghi urum nke na kabat. *A bat does not see even in the afternoon.*

ekeng (n) a python

ekese (adj) many; a lot of; much
  e.g. Ekese a bene ba Kororp be taak isai iruk. *Many people of Kororp have remained in other communities.*

ekikere (n) thought; idea
  e.g. Ekikere engo a kwa a M beke ngo a? *What is*

your thought about what I told you?
ekin [also aikin] (n) a joke; jest; tease
ekom (n) occiput (the back part of a head) e.g. Onerom quor or chorm anyiri a ekom. *The man has a long occiput.*
Ekornganaku (n) a Nigerian village of Kororp, in Oban District of Akpampka Local Government Area, Cross River State
ekon idio (n) a kind of pudding prepared by chopping cooked cocoyams into smaller pieces by dint of a small mortar stick and mixing the mass with rich palm oil and traditional spices, including pepper
Ekorn (n) known officially as Ekon I, a Cameroonian village of Kororp, in Mundemba Sub Division of Ndian Division, South West Region
Ekorn II (n) Ekon II, the official name of Erat
ekorki (n) bean pudding (usually cooked in plantain leaf)
ekoorn (n) a hornbill (a bird)
ekoort (n) black mamba
ekora! (intj) An expression of disgust or contempt
ekorng (n) a perewinkle
ekoro (n) a spade
ekoro anenen (n) a digging fork
ekpa (n) a bag
ekpa a duseeng (n) a travel bag
ekpa ubor (n) a handbag
ekpang (n) a farm (especially in an old farmland for planting food crops like cassava); a traditional dish of grated cocoyam or cassava cooked in foldded cocoyam or plantain leaves
ekpat (n) a bench made of a pole placed on two two-pronged sticks or bamboos
Ekpe [from Efi.] (n) a Kororp name
ekpaime (n) a bottle
ekpaime orworna (n) a snuff box (especially made of a small bottle)
ekpere (n) a thorny,wild yam
ekpontong (n) throat
ekpoor (n) a gorilla

Ekpor (n) a Kororp male name
ekpork (n) mangabey
ekpukpu ariet (n) bull frog
ekumambiere (n) bananas (native species harder than the ordinary species)
ekup (n) cooking
e.g. A ror ekup? *Do you know cooking?*
ekwe (n) a leopard; the highest, hierarchical traditional society in Kororp that represents the judiciary
ekweem (n) a fish
emaanna (n) behaviour
emem (n) peace
e.g. U normi u dung a emem. *It is good to live in peace.*
emorng (pro) his/her/it; his/hers/its (for singular possession)
e.g. 1. Enor emorng ndai. *This is his/her house.*
2. Emorng ndai? *Is this his/hers?*
embe (pro) their; theirs
e.g. 1. Enor embe ndior. *That is their house.*
2. Enor chor e re embe. *That house is theirs.*

emboon (pro) your; your (for singular possession)
e.g. 1. Enor emboon ndai? *Is this your house?*
2. Ebon chai emboon? *Is this goat yours?*
emuum (n) a dumb, the dumb
e.g. N dorni u neme na emuum. *I don't know how to discuss with a dumb.*
enaba (n) rainy season
e.g. U noormi tou borkor a enaba. *It is not advisable to plant crops in the rainy season.*
enami (n) a sheep
enang ukwak [from Efi., literally iron horse] (n) a bicycle
engo (pro) your; yours (in singular)
e.g. Enor engo ndai? *Is this your house?*
enghe (adj) yes
enini (n) an argument; a contention; a debate
e.g. 1. Uforn u reni a eninihai c. *There is no point for this argument.*
2. M biri de a enini na ngo. *I am not in a debate with you.*
enoom (n) a red duiker
enoork (n) a bush cat

enoorm (n) beauty (the appearance)
e.g. I biri de ma u taaina enoorm ebon. *We are not here to display our beauty.*
enoorn (n) the practice of going to the farm or "bush",
enop (n) an antelope
enor (n) a house, a building
enor a bian (n) a hospital
enor a buchoya (n) a bathroom
enor akam (n) a prayer house
enor a mkporkorbi (n) a prison
enor a nkwet (n) a school
enor a bokpiya (n) an orphanage
enor a echong (n) a storey building
enor a ekup (n) kitchen
enor a ereri (n) a church
enor a esop (n) a court
enor a irot (n) a shrine
enork (n) a fight; a war
enorn (n) cataract, a grey spot in the eye due to an infection
Enor Orbasi (n) a church
enor usaing (n) toilet
enu (n) a snake
enuum (n) a millipede

enyam (n) a monkey-eating eagle
enyi (n) an elephant
enyi a mini (n) (lit.: a water elephant) hippopotamus
enyorm (n) bush mango (fruits)
equook (n) hip
equn (n) foam
equn equn (adj) foamy
erang (n) a louse
Erat (n) known officially as Ekon II, a Cameroonian village of Kororp, in Mundemba Sub Division of Ndian Division, South West Region
ere (inf.v) is (some nouns that begin with "c" "e", "n" and "m" followed immediately by consonants go with "ere")
e.g. Chaap chor ere mmang? *Where is that animal?*
erequa (conj) if
e.g. Erequa a beghe kona nne. *If you arrive call me.*
ereri [from Efi.] (n) Sunday; church
e.g. 1. Ndaikwai Ereri. *Today is Sunday.*

2. N de a ereri aranghaquo. *I am in church right now.*
eretrik [from Eng.] (n) electricity
e.g. Ekese a isai ibon I chormi eretrik. *Many of our villages don't have electricity.*
erim (n) sweet yam
erop (n) soup (for eating fufu); "alligator" pepper (a spice); a juju in itself used to chew, spray and pray to kill
eroprain [from Eng.] (n) aeroplane
eromsin (n) heart; mind
erore (n) the habit of showing strong apetite for someone else's food
erork (n) a pit
erork a **usaing** (n) a pit latrine
erung (n) fog, mist, cloud
erung a mini (n) rain clouds
erung erung (adj) foggy, misty, cloudy
eruk (adj; pro) another, other (for nouns that begin with "e", "tch", "ch", "mba", "ne" or "nf")
e.g. 1.N kwaka u reu ebia eruk. *I want to buy another dog.*
2. Chang mmi chaap eruk. *Give me another meat.*
3. Nforokum eruk ndai. *This is another cotton.*
4. Mbakem eruk ereni. *There is no other short-cut.*
eruki (n) livestock, a domestic animal
e.g. Eebon e re eruki. *A goat is a domestic animal.*
eruk nchen (conj) perhaps
e.g. Eruk nchen o ri quai. *Perhaps he/she will not come.*
esaaing (n) virgina
esaaing a enor (n) family
esang (n) a barrel; a staff (especially of a titled person)
esang a dion (n) a gun barrel
esin (n) heart, mind
esing (n) a housefly
esop (v) court
esorke (n) the dry leaf (on a plant) that shakes vigorously in the slightest breeze
esorne (n) disgrace, shame; humiliation; embarrassment; dishonour
eta (n) cloth, clothes
etaing (adv) in, inside

e.g. 1. Ita imi I de etaing a okebe omi. *My clothes are in my box.*
2. Be re etaing enor. *They are inside the house.*

eating etaing (adv) inside

etaip (n) excessive praise; acclamation, a proclamation of someone as highly skilled or successful

eta a kornorngha (n) a bedsheet

eta a mumbai (n) breat wear

eti (adj) good, fine

etibe (n) thrift and loan, a meeting in which members contribute money in each sesssion and give to one member, according to an agreed plan

etighi (n) paw-paw

etoom (n) a drill

etoong (n) dizziness; wooziness; giddiness

etoowa (n) planting; sowing; cultivatation

eweep (n) air; breeze

ewok (n) a monkey

ewooka (n) a buffalo

ewoort (n) a giant rat (a rat mole)

Eworn (n) a male name

eworm (n) a cow

ewot (n) the habit of someone hanging around to be given food

ewuri (n) a waterfall, a rapid

eyain (n) a place, a plot, a spot, an area, a position (prep) where

e.g. Taina nne eyain a koomi munei mummi. *Show me where you have kept my oil.*

eyang (n) night hunting

e.g. O nyi eyang. *He's gone for night hunting.*

eyang ayip [from Eja.] (n) rainwater

eeyo (n) epoch, era, age

eeyo a dekwem (n) the age of enlightenment

eeyo a ikpesinghi (n) the dark ages

eyoo (n) sweet potatoe; gold colour; setting sun

eyop (n) honour, respect; recognition, credit

e.g. Nik i chang aye eyop. *Let us give him honour and respect.*

Ff

faam (v) boast
e.g. Kpara faam a biain ba a kemeni u sai. *Don't boast of what you cannot do.*
faaikere (v) argue, arguing; disagree, disagreeing
e.g. By faikere mmung ma, *What are you arguing about here?*
faain (v) feel depressed due to stress or something (consciously)
faain qua (v) commit suicide by consciously getting depressed, or starving onself, due to a problem
faait (v) go crazy due to a problem
e.g. N ka faait na ngo erekwua yire na nne ukwen. *I will go crazy with you if you continue to follow me with problems*
Faara [from Eng.] (n) a Reverend Father
e.g. Faara o nyi ereri. *The Reverend Father has gone to church.*
faibairai (v) lie
e.g. Kpara faibairai mmi. *Don't lie to me.*
(adj) to be fond of lying
e.g. Or faibairai kpai. *He/she is too fond on lying.*
faibaifaibairai (v) lying (telling lies)
e.g. A faibaifaibairai. *You are lying.*
fara (adv) fast, quick
e.g. Fara sai. *Do it fast.*
fara fara (adv) fast, quickly (for emphasis)
fat (v) barb, have a hair cut
e.g. *A kwaka u far niin ningo? Do you want to have a hair cut?*
Febuari [from Eng.] (n) February
febere (v) lighten, make to weigh less
e.g. Febere baikait baingo. *Lighten your body.*
fere (v) do a knot
feri (v) undo a knot
feri feri (adj) thin, flat
e.g. Chang mmi kababai ke feri feri. *Give me a thin plank.*
fiba (v) knot, fasten the knot,
(adj) tight (especially clothes), narrow (especially a path, road or door-way)

e.g. Eta chai e fiba kpai. *This clothes is too tight.*

fikiri (adv) really, actually; carefully, thoroughly, well

e.g. 1. A fikiri sai mmung duwom? *What job do you really/actually do?*
2. Fikiri sai duwom dor. *Do that work well.*
3. A fikiri buu aye? *Did you ask him/her well/carefully?*

(v) verify, cross-check, cross-validate, confirm

e.g. Seeng de fikiri na aye. *Go and verify/cross-check/confirm with him.*

fikiri fikiri (adv) truly, truly; really, really; verily, verily

e.g. 1. Fikiri fikiri mmung u tibe? *Really, really what happened?*
2. Fikiri, fikiri, M bek ngo nyenene.... *Verily, verily, I tell you again...*

fina (v) trouble, disturb, worry, bother, perturb

e.g. Kwen quo or fina ama kpai. *This child disturbs the mother too much.*

fiorb (v) suck, lick; kiss (repeatedly)

fioba (v) suck, lick; kiss (momentarily)

fiori (v) bruise, brush

e.g. N fiori iwain imi. *I have brushed by shin.*

fioror (v) float, floated, floating

fiort (n) the sound of sighing

e.g. A tornghor nyenene u fiort? *Are you starting again to make a sigh?*

fiorya (v) signal by quickly touching and rubbing on the body of someone with a finger or fingers

foon [from Engl.] (v) phone
(n) a phone

fore (v) to prosper

e.g. I ka fore, a din da Orbasi. *We shall prosper, in God's name.*

forere (v) open; to supernaturally cause someone to have a mishap

e.g. Forere disaing dingo. *Open your anus [which also figuratively means: "Expose yourself].*

fori (v) fall; collapse (e.g. into a pit)

e.g. Kak, kun N fori erork chai. *Nearly, I would have fallen into this pit*

forng (adj) open

e.g. 1. Kpara koom itum nyor forng. *Don't leave that door open.*
2. Or ya u koom ingwha imorng forng. *He/she is fond of keeping his mouth open.*

fornghene (v) open (slightly, especially the door or mouth)

Fraidai [from Engl.] (n) Friday

foto (v) photo, picture

fubi (v) pluck, pull out (quickly, e.g. a feather or a strand of hair)

fuum (v) beat; hit; strike; slap

e.g. Adutaina, kpara a fuum kwen quor. *Teacher, don't beat that child.*

fup (v) pluck (e.g. the feathers of a bird); cut too roughly (e.g. grass)

fururu (adj) round

fut (v) swell; swell up

fuu (adj) full

Ii

i (pro) we; we are
e.g. 1. I kpang ngo sanghana. *We heard you clearly.*
2. I quai. *We are coming.*
3. Ta p quai. *We have come.*
4. Ichaap i reni daing ma. *Animals are no longer here.*
5. Ichaap i ri quai daing ma. *Animals will not come here again.*

iba (n) an underwear
e.g. Iba a kwen a meng ndai? *Whose child's underwear is this?*

ibak (n) violence, wickedness; cruelty, evil; malice; malevolence,
e.g. Nik ibak. *Desist from wickedness.*

ibam (n) pockets (a specified number of)
e.g. Ibam iwang a chorm a eta engo chai? *How many pockets do you have in this your clothes?*

ibat (n) shoulders; hands of planatain or banana

ibet (n) a taboo; anathema; abomination

ibin (n) bass drum (usually big and long)

ibon na ibon (pro) amongst ourselves

ibor (n) hands

iboror (n) answer, answers; response, exponses

iboror a baikait (n) [lit.: body responses] senses (e.g. of smell, touch, etc)

ibubui (n) a wild pigeon

ibubui a orkat (n) a pigeon

ichai (n) streams

ichap (n) animals; meats

ichap a disaing (n) buttocks

ichap ichap (adj) meaty

ichari (n) bitter kola (plural with a specific number)

ichor (n) snails (a specified number of)

ichori (n) cane ropes

ichon (n) nose; catarrh

ichu a ikoon (n) testicles

ichu a orkat (n) acoconuts

idara [from Efi.] (n) jubilation, celebration

idiaii (n) a cutlass

idior (n) cocoyam leaves; a vegetable dish of cocoyam leaves

idomo [from Efi.] (n) a temptation; a trial

idot (n) juju

ifang (n) a parting between the two front teeth or incisors
ifiork (n) a trick, tricks; a tactic, tactics; a technique, techniques
ifum (n) a stool (e.g. of the kitchen)
iibat (n) Arithmetic, Mathematics
iibon (pro) ours
iiboon (pro) we; us
iifik (n) effort e.g. Korn iifik. *Put in an effort.*
iikpor (n) a hawk
iikpor enyam (n) a monkey-eating eagle
iinen (adj) direct e.g. Iinen ainain ndai. *This is the direct road/path.*
iinum (prep) behind (especially something or someone)
iiruum (n) plays; displays; concerts; performances; shows
ikakani (n) a fishing cage-trap made of bamboo
ikei (n) a farm in a new farmland for planting crops like plantains
ikinworng orworna (n) snuffbox especially made of a container like that of Rub
ikit (n) high jump

ikoi (n) an elbow
ikon (n) a type of seeds used for thickening soup, locally known as "egusi"
Ikondo-kondo (n) known officially as Ikondo-kondo I, a Cameroonian village of Kororp, near Mundemba in Ndian Division, South West Region
ikooma (n) a gizzard
ikoon (n) a scrotum
ikormor (n) a drum [a musical instrument]
ikorng esit [from Efi.] (n) sternum
ikot (n) a spoon
ikot a nenen (n) a fork
Ikpaan (n) (commonly spelt Ikpan) a Kororp river near Ekornganaku in the Cross River State of Nigeria
ikpaain (n) life; lifestyle
ikpai (n) the habit of beating especially little children; one of the divided parts or lip (especially of virgina)
ikpaii (n) rats; a terrible Kororp juju that is believed to kill massively
ikpainyin (n) a scorpion

ikpaisinghi (n) darkness, the dark
ikpakot (n) a shoe
ikpe (n) a case; a court case; a judgment
ikpeke (n) a curtain (used to conceal a bed)
ikpin (n) insistence; the habit of egging on someone
ikpin ikpin (adv) repeatedly, incessantly, ceaselessly
ikpo (n) ululation; applause; ovation
Ikpokobi (n) a deep valley, an abyss; a depression in Kororp into which hardened criminals were thrown
ikpor (adj) big, large; high (e.g. position)
e.g. 1. Ikpor a chap. *A big animal.*
2. O ning ikpor enyi. *He/she saw a large animal.*
3. Onerom quo or moori ikpor a kabara. *This man holds a high position.*
ikpork (n) slime (especially in stool)
iku (n) a bay duiker
ikung (n) chest
ikuuka (n) a wound
ikuyoork (n) an otter
ikwang (n) leaves; a vegetable or vegetables

imam (n) stinginess; miserliness; tightfistedness
imbaat (n) hoof
imbe (pro) their; theirs (for singular or plural possessions)
e.g. 1. Idiai imbe ndai. *This is their cutlass.*
2. Inung imbe i kwewi daing. *Their ears are also sharp.*
imbiet (n) a mongoose
imboon (pro) your; yours (plural pronoun, for singular or plural possessions)
e.g. 1. Idiaii imboon i rim. *Your cutlass is lost.*
2. Inung imboon i maaba? *Are your ears blocked?*
imboot (n) a wasp (one that resembles a mud wasp and can also be found in a house); a conk, a knock on the head
e.g. 1. Imboot i man aye. *A wasp has stung him/her.*
2. Or chang aye imboot. *He/she gave him/her a conk.*
imee [frim Efi.] (v) patience; tolerance; endurance; perseverance

imet (n) fuelwood, fire wood (in plurals)
imi (pro) my; mine (for plural possesions)
e.g. Inung imi i kwewi. *My ears are sharp.*
imorng (pro) his/her/its; his/hers/its (for singular or plural possessions)
e.g. 1. Idiaii imorng i kwewi. *His/her cutlass is sharp.*
2. Inung imorng i kwewi daing. *His/her ears are also sharp.*
imum (n) a smile
imuum (n) dumbness; a dumb
inang (n) bamboos (made from oil palm or raffia palm)
i nango (n) [lit.: "and you too", as a response to greetings such as…] good morning; good night
inaani (n) a huge, wide rock buried in and/or spread in or on the ground
Inaani a Batake (n) a narrow rock at old Ekon that, like the name implies, runs up a hill like a ladder

Inaani Ayoyo (n) a large and magnificent rock on top of a hill, near the old village of Ekon
inanong (n) a wasp (small in size and mostly in the wild)
inaii (n) money (in singular form)
inaii a nkwet (n) pen; pencil
inen (n) a blue duiker
inain (n) tracks, paths, routes
inenn (adj) direct, straight ahead
inghwa (n) a mouth; boasting; a squirrel
ingwha a mumbai (n) a nipple
infiaim (n) a whistle (made of metal or plastic)
ingo (pro) your; yours (singular pronoun, for singular or plural possessions)
e.g. 1. Idiaii ingo i turi. *Your cutlass is blunt.*
2. Imet ingo ndai? *Are these your fire wood?*
inhi (adj) yes
ini a kpain (adv) in ancient times
ini echimini (n) fruiting season

ini nyor (adv) in earlier times; formerly; previously; a long time ago

in inh (adj) no; sorry

ini ini (adv) occasionally, intermittently, periodically, from time to time, now and then, once in a while

ini nyini (conj) once, once upon a time; on one occasion; some time ago

injinia (n) an engineer

inken (n) tilapia

inkene (n) a cockroach; a stunted person (a figurative expression for)

inoi (n) shea nuts, edible nuts that can be used also to produce edible oil

inoom (n) blue duikers (a specified number of)

inoorp (n) beans

inornoi (n) a finger

intem (n) a bead (usually "chu intem", "chu" meaning "kernel" or "seed"

intongho (n) a mud wasp

intork (n) a sand fly

inu (n) snakes (a specified number of)

inum (n) back, hind (adv) behind

inun (n) thorny, wild ropes used especially for weaving traditional fishing cage-traps

inung (n) ears; deafness
e.g. 1. Taina mmi inung ingo. *Show me your ears.*
2. Ore orne inung [lit.: *He/she is a person of deafness*] *He/she is a deaf*

inyai nyaii (n) a bush pig, a red river hog

inyai nyaii a orkat (n) a pig (domestic)

inyene [from Efi.] (n) wealth
e.g. Amene omi or re orne a inyene. *My father is a wealthy person.*

inyi (n) elephants (a specified number of)

irap a nen (n) eye lids

iroorp (n) languages
e.g. Ntem quo or tangha ekese iroorp. *This fellow speaks several languages.*

irot (n) juju

iruk (n) another (for nouns beginning with "i")
e.g. Chang mmi idiaii iruk. *Give me another cutlass.*

irum (n) a parrot

isaaing a inor (n) families (a specified and an unspecified number of)

isat (n) a net put across a river to catch fish
isiin (n) roots
isin enyin [from Efi.] (n) jealousy
isio [from Efi.] (adj) different
e.g. Iiboon na mbe i bura isai isio. *We and they come from different villages.*
isop (n) a fine
isosoka (n) a weaver bird
isookoro (n) oranges (a specified number of)
isung (n) a messenger
isuwi (n) veins
itai (n) calf (of a leg)
itaim (n) advice; counsel; recommendation; proposal; suggestion
itam (n) a cap; a hat
ita a mumbai (n) breat wears
itemi (n) curses; wishes of misfortune
itorn (n) shame, shyness; embarrassment, disgrace
e.g. 1. Onerom quo or chormi itorn. *This man has no shame.*
2. Kpara a baquai itorn a enor chai. *Don't bring disgrace to this house.*
itort (n) a bird
itort a kakam (n) a clock bird
itort a ekai (n) a palm bird
itort a orkat (n) a cattle egret
itut (n) pile (an illness of the anus)
ituum [from Efi.] (n) a door
iwa (n) cassava
iwain (n) shin
iwok (n) monkeys (a specific number of)
e.g. O buut iwok iwaan. *He shot two monkeys.*
iwom (n) works; duties; functions; jobs; occupations; professions, careers; vacancies, openings
iworm (n) cows (a specified number of)
iyonoi (n) star; a whistle (made through the mouth)
e.g. 1. Ket iyoyoni a echong. *Look at a star in the sky.*
2. N dorni u qun iyoyoni. *I don't know how to blow a whistle.*

Jj

"J" does not begin a word, except the foreign ones below, but the sound is distinct in the words where it appears.

Jaman (n) Germany; a euphemism for a strong and stoical person.
e.g. 1. Orkat kwo o tungi Jaman. *This white is from Germany.*
2. Morngkwo amamang a Jaman. *This one is really a stoical person.*
Januari [from Eng.] (n) January
Jekorb (n) Jacob
Jises (n) Jesus
Jisors (n) Jesus
Jorn (n) John
Josef (n) Joseph
Jurai [from Eng.] (n) July
e.g. Jurai or norba mini. *July rains.*
Juun [from Eng.] (n) June

Kk

ka (inf. v) shall; will
e.g. 1. N ka qai. *I shall come.*
2. Or ka qai. *He/she will come.*

kaakpaai (n) tiredness
e.g. Kaakpaai kai sai a m be fara buki. *It is tiredness that caused me not to wake up early.*

kak (v) crawl, creep
e.g. Kwen omi or tornghor u kak. *My child has started to crawl.*

(n) a little
e.g. Korn munork kak. *Add salt a little.*

kaka (v) kneel
e.g. Kaka norom. *Kneel.*

kaainene (adj) clear; obvious; unambiguous; comprehensible; sparkling (usually water)

kaaineenee (v) filter (repeatedly)

kaaini (v) clear, for a river, stream, water in a container or any naturally clear liquid to become clear after the dirt in it has settled down

kaaka (v) climb unto someone's back to be carried; carry someone on one's back

kaaka kaaka (v) to be carried on someone's back, to carry someone on one's back
e.g. A ka kaaka kaaka? *Will you be carried on the back?*

kaaki [from Eng.](n) shorts (as opposed to trousers)

kaan (v) play out an oracle to tell the cause of a mishap (e.g. Kaan chuum")

(n) a pad used for carrying a load on the head

kaana (n) a branch (e.g. of a tree; of learning); a tributary
e.g. 1. Kana kor ke qua. *That tree branch is dead.*

kana ka dukpewi (n) a subject

kaani (v) separate a quarrel or fight
e.g. Kaani enork chor. *Separate that fight.*

kaankaii (n) a bitter lesson
e.g. Be taina ibon kaankaii. *They showed us a bitter lesson.*

kaana ka orkekei (n) palm frond

kaan ka ubor (n) palm (of the hand)

kaan ka uwon (n) sole (of the foot)

kaap (v) take sides with someone, especially in a quarrel

e.g. Or ya u kaap amene ormorng. *He is fond of taking sides with his/her father.*

kaat (v) freeze

e.g. Ayain chai e newi kpai, N ka kaat. *This place is too cold, I will freeze.*

kababai (n) plank, flat, sawn wood mostly for making doors and furniture

kababai ka buyeri [lit.: writing plank] (n) arm board; blackboard

kabai (n) carbide

kabat (n) afternoon

kabaat (n) standing (position); rank, position or post

e.g. 1. Or ya kabaat. *He/she is fond of standing.*
2. A mori kabaat nkaini ma? *Which position do you hold here?*

kabara (n) standing (position); rank, position, level

kabere (v) twist or distort especially a story or facts

e.g Kpara a kabere ukwen umi. *Don't distort my statement.*

kabia (n) potto

kabinta [from Eng.](v) carpenter

kachang (n) a gift

e.g. Kachang kaingo ndai. *This is your gift.*

kai (prep) this (always coming at the end of a sentence)

e.g. Katana kai. *This side.*

kaiba (v) take enema

e.g. U tap niet dio n na kaiba. *It is up to ten years now, I have not taken enema.*

kaibain (n) the earth, the universe, the world

kaibait (adv) up

e.g. Ket kaibait. *Look up.*

(prep) up

e.g. Ket kaibait ka yhion. *Look up the mountain.*

kaibait ka orkpa (adv) upriver

e.g. N dunghi kaibait ka orkpa. *I live upriver.*

kain (v) pour/fill a liquid into a container with a small opening e.g. A kemeni u kain munei a ekpaime? *You can't fill oil into a bottle?*

kainaii (n) a stick; a tree; wood

kainaii ka usaing (n) a traditional toilet made of a big round stick crossed on two forked sticks; latrine, toilet (now used generally for)

kainene (v) filter (momentarily)

e.g. A ini a bumork, kainene mini a ba chorn. *In times of illnesses, filter water before you drink.*

kainn (v) resemble; take after

e.g. Kainn mmi a kwa a sai. *Resemble me in what you do.*

kainni (v) resemble; take after

e.g. O kainni amene ormorng. *He resembles his father.*

kaibin (n) blackness

kaibini (n) charcoal

kaichim (n) a noise; din; sound

e.g. Kechim kor ke tunghi mmang? *Where is that noise coming from?*

kaik (v) go

kaikaire (v) cause to escape, caused to escape

e.g. Meng o kaikaire chap chor? *Who caused that animal to escape?*

kaikpaait (n) cocoyam

kaikpain (n) a tree hyrax

kaikpaing (n) wriggling in bed, struggle to get free

kaikpiiya (adv) face-down

e.g. Norngha kaikpiiya. *Lie/sleep face down.*

kaikwai (n) a thorn

kaikwai ka ekwem (n) fish bone

kaikwait (n) a break from work for a whole day (sometimes but not always associated with lazy people)

kain (v) resemble

e.g. Kain ormwha a duseng. *Resemble your mother in walking.*

kainaii (n) a tree; a stick

kaini (v) resemble; looks like

e.g. Or kaini ama ormorng a duseeng. *She resembles her mother in gait.*

kainimini (n) sweat, perspiration

kainimini kainimini (adj) sweaty, sticky

kaira (v) set or shake one into action that had

been suspended or stop; shake something that is hanging or placed precariously

kairaii (n) oil palm

kairaii ka orkat (n) pineapple

kairaisin [from Eng.] (n) kerosene

kairuk (adj) another (for nouns beginning with "ke", "ka", "kor" or "ko")

e.g. Chang mmi kaikpait kairuk. *Give me another cocoyam.*

kaisaisaing (n) fontanel

kaisimi (n) the chaff from smashed oil palm nuts

kaisin (n) liver

kaiyaaim (n) wake-keeping, vigil night, night before an important day

kaiyaiba (n) wandering

kaiyini (n) a boil

kak (n) a bit, a little; nearly, almost

e.g. 1. Kon munork kak. *Put salt a bit.*
2. Boorng kak. *Wait a little*
3. Kak kun N nor. *I nearly would have fallen.*

(v) crawl

e.g. Kwen omi ortornghor u kak. *My child has started walking.*

kakak (n) crawling

e.g. Kwe kwo or na tornghor kakak. *This child has not started crawling.*

kakaka (n) a giant pangolin

kakam (n) plantain (tree or bunch)

kaki (v) set down a load carried on the back

e.g. Kaki ekpa chor. *Set down the bag.*

kakpak (n) a forked stick, a two-pronged stick used for holding up a pole or poles

kakpaat (n) a foot; a footprint

kakang (n) quill; a hook to hold a lamp

kakpai (n) a comb

kakpak (n) stick with two prongs for crossing poles

kakwai (n) biomass of fallen trees that cause obstruction

kamaat (n) a scar

kamana (v) claim, seize, arrogate to oneself

e.g. Or ya u kamana bukorn baikait. *He/she likes to claim strength.*

kameng (pro) whose

e.g. Kakam ka meng ndai? *Whose plantain is this?*

kamkpang (n) smallest size tilapia type found mostly in small streams

kan (v) refuse; refute, repudiate (e.g. an accusation), exonerate; move along a branch, cross-bar or some other suspended narrow object

e.g. 1. A keme u kan baikait a ukwen quu? *Can you exonerate yourself in this issue?*

2. Or keme u kan a buuna ba kainaii kor. *He/she can move along the branches of that tree.*

kamarin (n) gamalin

kana (v) quarrel, wrangle, squabble

kananau (n) scabies

kanai (n) insult

kanaat (n) madness (state)

kanari (n) palm frond

kang (adj) big (always preceded by "bu" [real]

e.g. Enyi, bu kang! *An elephant, real big!*

kangkang (adj) difficult; serious

e.g. U de biain ba kangkang M ba keme usai chuna dowom dor. *It was a difficult thing before I was able to finish that work.*

(adv) seriously

e.g. Be quop aye kang-kang. *They beat him/her seriously.*

kanghi (adj) big (always precided by any a noun or pronoun)

e.g. A kanghi. *You are big.*

kankanghana (n) spirit; soul

kantak (n) insect

kann (v) send a message

e.g. A kann mbe? *Have you sent them a message?*

karam (n) grass; weeds

kari (n) gari, food made of cassava flour

karia (n) yam

karorn (n) gallon

kasak (n) rattle (a musical instrument)

katai (n) arrow

e.g. Kakai ka Orbasi. *The arrow of God.*

katakis [from Eng.] (n) Cathechist

katan (n) the uppermost part of the barn or shelf mainly for storing and for slow and long-term drying wood and other items in the kitchen

katana (n) side, area, quarters

e.g. N dorni katana kor. *I don't know that area.*

94

katchang (n) a gift
e.g. M mori ngo katchang. *I owe you a gift.*

katchang ka Orbasi (n) God's gift, natural gift, talent

kating (adj) alone, lonely
e.g. 1. M biri re kating. *I'm not alone.*
2. Nik mmi kating. *Leave me alone.*
(n) loneliness
1. Kating ke ka choon nne. *Loneliness will kill me.*
(v) Does it mean…? Could it mean…?Is it because…?
e.g. 1. Kating o quai? *Does it mean he/she has come?*
2. Kating a ntak a kanghi? *Is it because you are big?*

kawa (n) a short-snouted crocodile

kawat (n) a hoop; a wheel; a steering

keche (n) a gossip; backbiting; the act of gossiping or backbiting; a rumour

kediimi (n) diving

kee (v) is not; have not, will not
e.g. 1. Kemet kee reni. *There is no piece of fire wood.*
2. Kaisin kee noormi. *Refusal is not good.*
3. Kenweng kor kee ri quai daing. *That Guinea fowl will not come again.*

keeket (n) gawking, gaping
e.g. Or ya kpai keeket. *He/she is too fond of gawking.*

keem (v) cut, take a short cut or an unpopular route
e.g. Nik I keem ma ko I fara dion. *Let us cut here si we can reach fast.*

keen (v) peel (especially cocoyam)

keereek (n) rest, leave, holiday, vacation
e.g. Niet ninaan ndai, n na chorma kereek. *It is three years now, I have not had a vacation.*

keeyeei (n) shouting, barking; the act or habit of shouting or barking at someone or people
e.g. Or ya kpainkang keeyeei. *He/she is too fond of shouting.*

kekere (adj) too; too much, too many
e.g. Beken bor be chawi kekere. *Those visitors are too many.*

kekeme (n) ember

kekpeek (n) limping

kem (adj) enough; fitting; in adequate measure (e.g. salt)
e.g. 1. U kem. *It's enough.*
kembeet (n) foolhardiness
e.g. Utor a kai kembeet a? *Why this type of foolhardiness.*
keme (inf.v) able to, can; capable of
e.g. 1. A keme u nwam donuna dor? *Can you carry that load?*
2. A keme kenweye? *Are you capable of engaging in a race?*
kemeni (inf.v) cannot, unable, incapable
e.g. Or kemeni u baat. *He/she cannot stand.*
keme (v) can, able, capable
kemet (n) a piece or log of fire wood
kemika [from Eng.] (v) a chemical
e.g. N yani u dia daria da bai sai na kemika. *I don't like to eat food made of chemical.*
ken (v) stay the night
e.g. N ka ken ma. *I will stay the night here.*
kenemi (n) secondary forest, forest plot
e.g. 1. Eyain chai ere kenemi. *This area is a secondary forest.*
2. Kenemi kaimi ndai. *This is my plot.*
kenweng (n) Guinea fowl
kenwep (n) a small fish with the shape and colour of golden barb but found mostly in small streams
kenweye (n) running; race; an escape
kere (v) is [i.e. is available](nouns that begin with "ka", "ke", "ko" and "ku" go with "kere"); there is; think, thinking, thought
e.g. 1. Kainaii kere. *There is a stick.*
2. N kere ma or ka quai. *I think (or thought) that he/she will come.*
kere kere (adv) very well; strongly; hard
e.g. 1. N neme na aye kerekere. *I discussed with him/her very well.*
2. Korm donuna dor kerekere. Tie that load strongly.
3. Mamana ubor umorng kerekere. *Press his/her hand hard.*
kerei (n) a masquerade

keri (v) look for, looking for, search for; think, thought
e.g. 1. A keri meng? *Who are you looking for?*
2. A keri a mmung u tibe? *What did you think has happened?*

keriri (v) looking for, searching for
e.g. A keriri mmung? *What are you looking for?*

ket (v) look; observe; take care of
e.g. 1. Ket ndaing. *Look here.*
2. Ket u tibe ndaing. *Observe what is happening here.*
3. Tum ket kwen quor. *Take good care of that child.*

ketei (n) a trap, a snare

keyei (n) the moon

keyeri (adv) face-up
e.g. Norngha keyeri. *Lie/sleep face-up*

keyebi (n) an imitation, a counterfeit (something imitated)
e.g. Inaii nyi i re keyebi. *This money is counterfeit.*

keyeyebi (n) an imitation (the act of imitating)
e.g. Ini iruk keyeyebi ke noormi. *Sometimes imitation is not advisable.*

ki (prep) this
e.g. Kini ki. *This ant.*
(v) has
e.g. Kini ki dong nne. *An ant has bitten me.*

kibain (n) an injunction, an announcement; a spell
e.g. 1. N ka korn kibain u tire aye dumeen. *I will put an injunction to stop him/her from drinking.*
2. Or chorm kibain. [lit.: *He/she has a spell*] *He/she is under a spell.*

kibin (n) a massive come-together for an important celebration, a conference; a retreat
e.g. I chorm kibin a uyei uruk. *We have a conference next week.*

kichikinyam (n) tse-tse fly

kichu (n) a plot, a clique; a delibration, a consultation
e.g. Nik i chorma quorna a kichu. *Let's have a little deliberation.*

kidiort (adj) something imature
e.g. Kidiort ka kakam. *Imature plantain.*
(n) imature type.

e.g. Kakam kai ata ata a kidiort. *This plantain is a really imature type.*
kifokoro (n) a lung
kifu (n) a herb used especially for medicine or juju
kiichin [from Eng.] (n) a kitchen
kiini (n) an ant (especially the soldier type)
kikaim (n) a portion, a place, a spot, a part
kikpuk (n) a lump, a swelling
e.g. Or chorm quorna a kikpuk a imum. *He/she has a little lump in the back.*
kikpe (n) an apology, request for forgiveness
e.g. A mori mmi kikpe. *You owe me an apology.*
kikuku (n) feebleness, a condition of having no strength to fight or do hard work
kikukum (n) a stump (of a tree)
kikuut (n) a ramshackle or dilapidated building (building near collapse)
kimaam (n) a masquerade that waylays and chastens stubborn children
kimaam ka ben (n) dragonfly
kimbokoro (n) a skull; a brain (a eupphemism for intelligence)
e.g. 1. Meng or kwa kimbokoro ka chap chai? *Who picked the skull of this animal?*
2. Or chorm kimbokoro. *He/she has a brain.*
kinchung (n) otter, an aquatic animal known for destroying fish cage-traps
kindumi (adj) rotten, smelly (especially meat)
e.g. Kindumi ka chaap chai? *This rotten/smelly meat?*
(n) rotten meat
e.g. 1. Kindumi ki noormi. *Rotten meat is not good.*
2. N yani udia kindumi. *I don't like to eat rotten meat.*
kinkorng (n) backbone, spinal cord
kinsang (n) a slim person (adj) slim
e.g. Amamang a kinsang ka orne! *A typically slim person!*

kinsorng (n) the first flow of palm wine (usually but not always sweet)
(adj) imature crop (especially casavva)
e.g. N yani kinsorng ka iwa. *I don't like immature cassava.*

ki (v) is (nouns that begin with "ki"and "ti" go with "ki re")

kire (n) reluctance, unwillingness, lack of enthusiasm
e.g. N chorm quorna a kire u dion a etibe emboon. *I feel a bit of reluctance to join your trift and loan.*

kire kire (adv) reluctantly
e.g. A seng nning ndai kire kire? *Why are you walking so reluctantly?*

kiro (n) behaviour
e.g. Ornaton quor or chorm ankorn a kiro. *That woman has a difficult behaviour.*

kirorng (n) a convoy; a group; a crowd
e.g. 1. U normi u seeng a kirorng. *It is advisable to move in a convoy.*
2. U normi u rung a kirorng. *It is advisable to live in a group.*
3. Mmung kirorng ndior? *What crowd is that?*

kiriing (n) a long basket used for carrying load

kiruk (adj) another (for nouns beginning with "ki")

kisima (n) a small drum blocked at the open end with a short, carved banana stem to produce a high pitched sound

kisiya (n) stupidity; foolish acts or jokes

kita [from Eng.] (n) a guitar

kito (n) morning
e.g. Quai a enor aimi na kito. *Come to my house in the morning.*

Kitork (n) the first settlement of Kororp

kitingha (n) clitoris

kitu (n) foolishness; imbecility
e.g. U noormi u rung ikpain a kitu. *It is not good to live a life of foolishness.*

kitum (n) a hut

kiworni (adj) rotten
e.g. N diani kiworni ka chaap. *I don't eat rotten meat.*
(n) something rotten

ko (conj) so; so that, in order that; before, by the time

e.g. 1. Ko mmung? *So what?*
2. Tang duchorn ko be be kpang. *Speak softly so that they don't hear.*
3. Fara dia ko be quai. *Eat fast before they come.*
4. Ko be re quai ta ini i kaik. *By the time they arrived it was late.*

kobobiri (n) sheet (e.g. of paper)
e.g. Chang mmi kobobiti ka nkwet kaini. *Give me one sheet of paper.*

koboka (v) runoff; standing or running rain water

kobom (n) a basket

koboop (n) a wing
e.g. U kaini ngha itort nyor i nwen koboop. *It looks like that bird has broken a wing.*

kobot (n) whiteness

kocho (n) two sticks one, of which is beaten on the other to produce music

kochok (n) shouting (the sound, act or habit of)

kochoka (n) shouting (the sound of)

kochook (n) crowned eagle

koduuba (n) hiding

e.g. Or re a koduuba. *He/she is in hiding.*

koi (n) thirst
e.g. Mbork, chang ne mini, n kwa koi. *Please, give me water, I am dying of thirst.*

koi ke nu (adj) thirsty
e.g. Koi ke nu nne. *I am thirsty.*

korfmen [from Eng.](n) government

korka (v) crow; boast; brag

kokpokpo (n) a nail (a metal piece); a vehicle (a euphemism for)
e.g. 1. Tum mora kokpokpo kor. *Hit that nail well.*
2. N deu kokpokpo. *I have bought a vehicle.*

koko (n) papa, daddy, a child's name for father; elder, a title for an elderly man; name-sake
e.g. 1. Koko, a ka dia biain? *Daddy, will you eat something?*
2. Koko Osere ta or yeen. *Elder Osere has already returned home.*
3. Offiong Ewon or de koko omi. *Effiong Eworn is my name-sake.*

kokot (n) face

kokuup (n) a broom made of a bunch-stock (used

in Kororp for sweeping especially wood ash from the fire place)

kokwop (n) scale (e.g. of a fish)

koma (v) kneel; pin (for instance a stick); imprison or jail someone

e.g. N ka koma ngo. *I will imprison you.*

kona (v) call, called; invite, invited

e.g. 1. Kona chang mmi aye. *Call him/her for me.*
2. Meng o kona ngo ma? *Who invited you here?*

kona quai (v) call, invite

e.g. Meng o kona quai ngo ma? *Who invited you here?*

kondoni (n) ripe bananas

kondoni ka kakam (n) ripe plantains

koni (v) remember, remembered; remind, reminded

konini (v) remembering, remembered; reminded

e.g. 1. Diet du re daikwai da i konini boman ba Jises. *Christmas is the day we are remeembering the birth of Jesus.*
2. A konini mmung? *What have you remembered?*

konkon (n) an owl

konou (n) chimpanzee

konkuun (n) placenta

e.g. Be nyi konkuun kami a onum Ekorn. *My placenta is buried at old Ekon.*

konum (n) dry season

e.g. Konum ke tori kpai mandai. *The dry season is too hot here.*

konumm (n) growth; development

konumwok (n) a red colobus monkey

konun (n) waist

kooi (v) cut, cutting, cut; stab, stabbing, stabbed (one thing/person or more things/people)

e.g. 1. A keme u kooi ankorn a koong ka kainaii kai? *Can you cut the hard bark of this tree?*
2. Meng or kooi kakaii ndior. *Who is cutting the tree like that?*
3. A ning orne a kanaat na idiaii nwei, ko or bere kooi ngo. *If you see a mad person with a cutlass run, so that he/she does not stab you.*

kook (v) set fish cage traps

e.g. Otrnwha or re kook munkanani. *Your mother*

has gone to set fish cage traps.
kooki (v) lose weight; grow thin
kooko [from Eng.]((n) cocoa
koom (v) keep; put
e.g. 1. Koom mmi doong dai a enor engo. *Keep me this parcel in your house.*
2. Koom dion dor a bukei. *Put that gun down.*
kooma (v) get onself imprisoned
e.g. A kwaka u kooma? *Do you want to be imprisoned?*
koomkpok (n) a tadpole
koomkpoon (n) a club, a huge stick
koon (v) read; call continually; call loudly continuously especially to resuscitate a dying person
e.g. A roni u koon? *Don't you know how to read?*
koona (v) refer to; calling
e.g. 1. A koona mbe a ning? *What do you refer them to?*
2. A koona meng? *Who are you calling?*
koong (n) a shell (of a tortoise, a snail or a nut); a peeling (of a banana, a plantain, a cassava); a skin or a hide (of an animal), a bark (of a tree)
koong ka ingwa (n) [lit.: the shell of the mouth] lip (of the mouth)
kooni (v) faint, fainted; farmish, farmished
(n) refuse dump
koonum (n) growth
koonuuka (n) bending position
e.g. Koonuuka ke koorni nne ayikwai antak a dunum. *Bending position is difficult for me these days because of old age.*
koori (n) evening
koork (v) crow; boast; brag
koorka (v) crowing; boasting, bragging
e.g. 1. Unorn quor u koorka mmung? *Why is that cock crowing?*
2. A koorka yonini mmung ma? *What are you bragging about here?*
koorm (n) a fence
koorma (v) rub oneself
koorn (v) serve (e.g. drinks; join; pack; wear, wearing
e.g. 1. Koorn munok mor. *Serve that wine.*

2. A roni u koorn busang? *Don't you know how to join pipes?*
3. Ta a tornghor u koorn ekpa engo? *Have you started to pack your bag?*
4. Ta n tornghor u koorn ita imi a diet. *I have started wearing my Christmas clothes.*

koorfi [from Eng.](n) coffee

koorokoro (n) fidgetting; restlessness; uneasinesss

e.g. Kwen kwo or ya kpai koorokoro. *This child is too fond of restlessnesss.*

kooroon (n) redness; fairnesss of skin

koort (n) neck, greed

koort ka ubor (n) wrist

koort ka uworn (n) ankle

koot (v) beat (especially a drum)

e.g. Or roni u koot ikormor. *He/she does't know how to beat the drum.*

kor (v) take (pre) that

e.g. 1. Kor duwam uka. *Take a part for now.*
2. Katana kor. *That side.*

kora (v) be swept away by water

e.g. Ekpa emorng e kora. *His/her bag has been swept away by water.*

korbor (v) frequent; fond of

e.g. Bumork bu korbor ngo, bu ba ngo a akpatire. *If an illness frequents you, it takes you eventually.*

korchor (n) adultery (in singular)

e.g. U noormi u korn korchor. *It is not good to commit adultery.*

korere (v) twist, bend, meander; beat about the bush; cause to be swept away by water

korkporka (n) a brownish tooth due to prolonged coating from food particles and lack of dental care

korkworn (n) avoidance; escape

korm (v) rub (e.g. someone with oil); tie, tied; build, built

kormi (v) tying, tied; building, built; rubbing, rubbed

e.g. A kormi mmung a ubor? *What have you tied on your hand?*

kormbani [from Eng.](n) company

kormkpork (n) a lizard
kormorn (n) young, yellow palm fronds
e.g. *A ini a diet, bene be na korki kormorn a neteke membe.* At Christmas, people often hang young, yellow palm fronds on their verandahs.
kormborm (n) bullfrog
kormkporn (n) stomach
korn (v) put, include (e.g. something, a name or someone); commit (e.g. adultery); wear (e.g. clothes); take (especially snuff); set (e.g. fire on a farm plot); make (e.g. fire (e.g. under a pot)
e.g. 1. *Korn din dimi mandior.* Include my name there.
2. *Korn kwen kwor eta.* Wear that child clothes.
3. *U noormi u korn dion ekpang nyidior.* It is not good to set fire on a farm plot loke that.
4. *Korn dion a dorkorng dor.* Make fire under that pot.
korna (v) put, included (e.g. something, a name or someone); committed (e.g. adultery); wore (e.g. clothes); took (especially snuff); set (e.g. fire on a farm plot); made (e.g. fire (e.g. under a pot)
korna...buqun (v) impregnated
korn buqun (v) to impregnate, to cause a woman to become pregnant
korn choop (v) put on weight
e.g. *A tornhor u korn choop.* You are beginning to put on weight.
korn...unem (v) bless
e.g. *Korn mmi unem, Omuna.* Bless me, Lord.
korni (adj) strong; difficult; hard
e.g. 1. *Onerom quo or korni.* That man is strong.
2. *Duwom dor du korni.* That job is difficult.
3. *Kui kor ke korni.* That bone is hard.
(Note that change in accent on the verb changes these words into the opposite)
(adj) not strong; not difficult; not hard
e.g. 1. *Onerom quor oor korni.* That man is not strong.
2. *Duwom dor duu korni.* That job is not difficult.

3. Kui kor kee korni. *That bone is not hard.*
korni dono (adj) stubborn
e.g. Kwen quor or korni dono. *That child is stubborn.*
korngha (n) cough; phlegm
kornorm (n) dance, dancing
kornorn (adv) under
e.g. Aikpaimai e re a kornorn ka okpokoro quor. *There is a bottle under that table.*
kornorngha (n) a bed
kornornghi (n) a maggot
e.g. Or ror kornorm ngha kornornghi. *He/she is as good at dancing as a maggot.*
kornoort (n) a nail (of a finger or toe)
kornyorni (n) spittle; slime
e.g. Meng o tura kornyorni kai? *Who spat out this spittle?*
korobi (n) an area of very high animal activity, especially elephants, characterised by large tracks or salt licks
koroi (n) a wound, a sore
korokiri (n) invectives, abusive language; the act of using invectives or abusive lanuage on someone
e.g. Or ya korokiri. *He/she is fond of using invectives.*
korongha (n) vapour; steam; breath
e.g. Korongha ka dorkorng ke fuum aye a dunyor. *The vapour from the pot has hit him/her on the face.*
korou (n) weight; credibility; integrity
e.g. 1. Norborn ne chorm korou. *Cartridges have weight.*
2. Erequa orborn or de na ibon, korsorwa kaibon ke ka chorma korou. *If the chief is with us, our meeting will have credibility.*
3. Onerom quo or chormi korou. *This man does not have integrity.*
korn (v) put
kornorn (adv) down
e.g. Or nyi kornorn ndor. *He is going down there.*
(prep) down; under
kornorn ka orkpa (adv) downriver
e.g. N dunghi kornorn ka orkpa. *I live down river*
korp [from Eng.](n) cup
korntorng (n) rattan (in singular)

e.g. Korntorng ke chorm bukwai. *Rattan has thorns.*

koror (v) look
e.g. 1. Koror, kpara kwaka mmi ukwen. *Look, don't look for trouble with me.*
2. Koror ndaing! *Look here!*
3. Koror mbe ndor. *Look at them there.*

Kororp (n) (commonly spelt "Kororp") an ethnic group that straddles Cameroon and Nigeria and which neignbours Ejagham on both sides and Oroko only in Cameroon

korsorba (adj) boilded
e.g. N ya u dia kakam korsorba. *I like to eat plantain boilded.*

korsorwa (n) a chair; a seat, a sofa; sitting, meeting

korsorwa ka duborn (n) the throne

kortori (n) ember, a piece of burning fuelwood, (euphemism) hot temper

kortorng (n) smoke

kortortort (n) heat, fever, (figuratively) the habit of being always in a rush

korum (n) ordour, smell

koryoror (n) wandering (especially unecessary)
e.g. Tire koryoror. *Stop wandering.*

kot (v) cut (especially into short or small pieces)

kotchok (n) noise, din, loud noise

kotchook (n) crowned eagle

kotchou (n) dance

kotoka (n) squatting (the act or position of)

kotchuka (n) assembly, congregation, gatherering

kotom (n) a container

ko ude (conj) neither...nor
e.g. Ibon asik isai, ko ude mboon. *It is neither we nor you that did it.*

ko utung mandior (conj) in order that

kowonini (n) a wild, hot spice of very small seed popularly called bush pepper

kpa (v) cut one thing or stab one person once

kpaai adj) too
1. Suka ornyenghe kpaai. *The sugar is too sweet.*

kpai (inf. v) tired; to be more than
e.g. 1. N kpai. *I am tired.*

2. N kpai ngo. *I am more than you.*

kpaiik (v) show off (especially beauty); to spill from a container from shaking (for liquid to)

kpaik (v) sew, stitch

kpa ikpo (v) ululate; applaud

e.g. Batoon be dor u kpa ikpo. *Women know how to ululate.*

kpai nkang (adj) too much; too fond of; beyond compare.

e.g. 1. Uyire ungo u kpainkang. *Your insistence is too much.*

2. Bukong dono bumorng bu kpainkang. *His stubborness is beyond compare.*

kpain (v) stay long; live, live long; to be alive

kpaing (v) wriggle (especially in bed); struggle or wrestle to get free

e.g. 1. A ya u kpaing a kornorngha. *You are fond of wriggling in bed.*

2. Yiiuut I yani u kpaing a waya. *A water chevrotain is not fond of wrestling in a trap.*

kpainghi (v) does not (or do not) wriggle or wrestle

e.g. Yiuut i kpainghi a waya. *A Water chevrotain does not wrestle in a trap.*

kpainn (adj) ancient; long ago

e.g. Bene ba kpainn. *Ancient people.*

(adv) long ago; since

e.g. 1. Or ba rik a duse kpainn. *He returned home long ago.*

2. Or ba dion ma kpainn. *He has arrived here since.*

kpaip (v) catch in air

kpairere (v) set down (e.g. a bag), help someone down from a height

kpang (v) hear; listen to; taste; smell

e.g. 1. M biri kpang u tibe. *I did not hear what happened.*

2. Kpang mmi. *Listen to me.*

3. Kpang nduk chior bor munork mu nkem. *Taste the soup to know whether the salt is OK.*

4. Kpang korum kor.*Perceive that smell.*

kpak (v) mark out; ask for a debt.

e.g. 1. Kpak uben ekpang engo. *Mark out your farm boundary.*

2. Kpak maruum mengo. *Ask for your debt.*

kpaka (v) wedge; button

e.g. 1. Kpaka itum nyior. *Wedge that door.*

2. Tum kpaka orfornirem ongo. *Button your shirt well.*

kpaki (v) unbutton; unzip (adj) poor

e.g. Or kpaki. *He/she is poor.*

kpam (v) reveal (e.g. a secret); operate upon; to perform an utopsy on; to split (e.g. wood); tear or cut (especially cloth)

kpan (v) stop (e.g. someone from continuing an act); forbid

e.g. Kpan aye. *Stop him/her.*

kpanini (adj) selfish

e.g. Or kpanini. *He/she is selfish.*

kpangha (v) bolt, lock e.g. a door

e.g. Kpangha itum nyior. *Lock that door.*

(adj) acidic

e.g. Ben ba sookoro be kpangha. *Limes areacidic.*

kpanghi (v) undo the bolt; unhinge

e.g. 1. Kpanghi itum nyior. *Undo the bold of that door.*

2. Kpara kpanghi mmi batanbadiaat. *Don't you unhinge my jaw bones.*

kpara (inf. v) hang; don't

e.g. 1. Kpara eta chor ma. *Hang that clothes here.*

2. Kpara quai uka. *Don't come yet.*

kpari (v) clear the throat; remove from hanging position (e.g. clothes); clarify

e.g. 1. Kpari koort. *Clear your throat.*

2. Mbork, kpari mmi ita nyor. *Please, remove those clothes for me.*

3. Kpari mmi ukwen kwu. *Clarify this point for me.*

kpaat (v) hang (e.g. many clothes)

e.g. Kpaat ita nyor a durik dor. *Hang those clothes on that rope.*

kpat (adv) until; all; completely

e.g. 1. Borng ma kpat n sibiri quai. *Wait here until I return.*

2. Or dia borkor bor kpat. *He/she has eaten all the food.*

kpaya (v) strike (e.g. a match); hit to destroy (especially a lock), break off

e.g. 1. U korni u kpaya ambaka uda ikang. *It is difficult to strike a wet match.*
2. Meng or kpaya dorkin dai? *Who destroyed this lock?*
3. Kana kor ke ka kpaya. *That branch will break.*

kpe (v) pay; beg for forgiveness, apologise to; preside over a case
1. Ta kpe aye maruum maingo? *Have you paid him your debt.*
2. Seeng de kpe aye. *Go and apologise to him/her.*
3. Meng or kpe ikpe nyor? *Who presided over that case?*

kpeek (v) limp; hobble

kpeem (v) beg something from

kpekpe (adv) all, completely
e.g. 1. Baquai kpekpe. *Bring all.*
2. Wiriri bien mini mor kpekpe. *Pour away that water completely.*

kpekpere (adj) every
e.g. A chorm u kpe munei a kpekpere a chiap a chooni. *You must pay a fee for every animal that you hunt.*

kpekpere a biain (n) everything

kpekpere a orne (n) everybody, everyone

kpeme (v) watch, watch over, guard, safeguard

kpemene (v) put ablaze

kpep (v) for fire to burst into flames; for a trap to move into a position that indicates that it has caught an animal

kpera (v) get down, climb down, reach

kpewere (v) teach; train; coach

kpewi (v) learn, study, practice, train in

kpii (v) open (e.g. ears, eye or eyes, a pan or box)

kpika (v) get interrupted, interrupt; restrain, control

kpikiri (v) teach someone a lesson; discipline; chastise, reprimand, rebuke
e.g. Be kpikiri aye, nkwor u sai a morng or tonrnghor kuba baikait bemorng. *They have taught him/her a lesson, that is why he/she is beginning to take his/her time.*

kpini (v) insist; persist

e.g. Kpara kpini. *Don't insist.*

kpini na (v) insist on, egg on

e.g. Kpini na aye ko o be china. *Egg on him/her so he/she does not forget.*

kpiya (v) cover (e.g. a pan, box, or a pit)

kpiiya (v) cover (e.g. oneself with a cloth); lie prostrate

e.g. 1. Erequa bioi bu nu ngo, kpiiya eta chor. *If you are feeling cold, cover that cloth.*

2. Erekwa etoong e nu ngo, kpiiya a bukei. *If you feel dizzy, lie prostrate.*

(adj) shut; dumbfounded

e.g. inwha imorng i kpiiya. *His/her mouth is shut.*

kpoi (v) peel (e.g. plantain); vimit, throw up

kpok (v) pluck or harvest (especially vegetables and fruits)

kpono (v) respect; honour

e.g. Achorm u kpono boonum. *You have to respect elders.*

kpononi (v) don't respect; don't honour

e.g. Ntak a kpononi boonum a? *Why is it that you don't respect elders?*

kpook (v) eat or suck a bone

kpoork (v) make (usually a fire)

e.g. A dor u kpoork dion? *Do you know how top make a fire?*

kpoowa (v) barking , (figuratively) shouting loudly

e.g.1. Ebia chor e kpoowa mmung? *Why is that dog barking.*

2. A kpoowa mmung ma, Ojom? *Why are you barking here, Ojom?*

kporba (v) hang (especially for safe keeping)

e.g. Kporba eta engo ma. *Hang your clothes here.*

kporbi (v) remove, for example clothes, from a hanging position

kpork (v) walk too slowly; dally, dawdle; jeer, boo

e.g. 1. Or ya u kpork duseeng. *He is fond of walking slowly.*

2. Erequa o dioni quai ma, kpork nor na aye. *If he/she comes in here, jeer at him/her.*

kporkere (v) open with a key; quickly make a fire

kporkpor (adv) forever; never

e.g. 1. A ka taak ma kporkpor? *Will you remain here forever?*
2. N di quai daing ma kporkpor. *I will not come here forever.*

kporkpor na kpor (adv) never; for ever and ever
e.g. 1. Mmi nyenene? kporkpor na kpor. *Me again? Never.*
2. Or yeyen ndior kporkpor na kpor. *He/she is departing for ever and ever.*

kporkpora (adj) every
e.g. Kporkpora orne enor orborn. *Everyone to the chief's palace.*

kporkporini (adv) always

kpori (v) pull down things (such as hanging ropes) from a height

kporiquai (v) come out en mass
e.g. Be kporiquai ngha bini. *They came ot en mass like ants.*

kpororo (adv) openly; clearly
e.g. N na sai seeng biain bumi kpororo. *I always do my things openly.*

kpoort (v) shave hair; remove thatches from a roof
e.g. 1. Koko, n ka kpoort nin. *Papa, I want to shave*
2. Or kpoort ekai enor emong. *He/she has removed the thatches of the roof of his house.*

kport (adv) only
e.g. N ning chaap chaini kport a nasona pak. *I saw one animal only in the National Park.*

kporya (v) peel off the skin of (e.g. banana, a toe, or healing wound)

kpou (v) bark repeatedly; (figuratively) shout loudly and repeatedly

kpowa (v) bark once; shout loudly (once)

kpuki (v) touch

kuba (v) hold; catch; take care of

kuba dara (v) [idiomatic] agree on a strategy; reach an agreement.
e.g. Kuba dara naaye. *Agree on a strategy with him/her.*

kuba baikait (v) to be careful, to take one's time

kuba dono (v) reach an agreement/final decision
e.g. Ta bu kuba dono a ukwen quor? *Have you reached an agreement on that issue yet?*

kubi (v) cooking
e.g. O kubi deesi. *She/he is cooking rice.*
kui (n) bone
kui ka dutang (n) a rib
kui ka equook (n) hip bone
kuk (v) count
kuka (v) wound (for example someone, an animal or a tree)
kum (v) stitch (e.g. thatches); weave (e.g. cloth)
kuma (v) momentarily pound the ground with the feet
kun (conj) then; otherwise; will have, would have
e.g. 1. Kun mmung u ka tibe? *Then what will happen?*
2. Kun M biri quai. *Otherwise I would not have come.*
3. Kun ta N dion. *I would have arrived.*
kunghi (v) exume (e.g. a corpse)
kup (v) cook
e.g. A kwaka u kup mmung? *What do you want to cook?*
kura (v) shake off (briefly, especially dirt, dust or tiny animals from)

kuraa (adv) act deliberately, voluntarily, out of one's volition
e.g. Mmi n kuraa sai. *I did it voluntarily.*
kuuka (v) have a wound
e.g. A kwaka u kuuka? *Do you want to have a wound?*
kuum (v) pound the ground repeatedly with the feet; to move about pounding the ground proudly
kuun (n) a tortoise; (figuratively) a cunning person
kuun ka mini (n) a turtle
kuut (v) shake off especially dirt, dust or tiny animals from
kuut baikait (v) urinate (a polite, euphemistic expression for), go to the bathroom
kuwiri (adj) short (always precided by a noun or a pronoun)
e.g. 1. A kuwiri. *You are short.*
kwa (v) die, died, dead; wither, withered; cost
e.g. 1. Kpara sai aye or fara kwa.
Don't let him/her die soon.

2. Daria dai de kwa munaii munwang? *How much does this food cost?*
kwaa (v) pick
kwak (v) want
e.g. M biri kwak u ning aye daing. *I don't want to see him/her again*
kwaka (v) search, look for; want, need
e.g. 1. A kwaka mmung? *What are you looking for?/ What do you want/need?*
2. A kwaka u nyi mmang *Where do you want to go?*
kwaki (v) don't want; don't like
e.g. N kwaki u ning ngo ma daing. *I don't want to see you here again*
kwanaka (adv) later; in a little while, for a while; soon; a little
e.g. 1. N ka ning ngo kwanaka. *I'll see you later.* N ka rik kwanaka. *I'll return soon.*
2. Be ka re ma kwanaka. *They will be here in a little while.*
3. Deek ma kwanaka. *Rest here for a while.*
4. N yani aye nke kwanaka. *I don't like him/her even a little.*
kwei (v) sweep; clear (everything)

kwen (n) a child
kwen a bak (n) a baby
kwen a buman (n) maternal nephew or niece
kwen a buwon (n) paternal nephew or niece
kwen a nkwet (n) a pupil, a student
kwen a enor (n) a servant
kwen a okpiya (n) an orphan child
kwen a okpo (n) an assistant to a hunter (whose responsibility is to help carry the meat and other items)
kwen a ornaton (n) a girl; a daughter
kwen a ornerom (n) a boy; a son
Kwen a Orbasi (n) a child of God; the Son of God
kwen a orboror (n) a small drum, smaller than orboror
kwen a orchorn (n) a baby
e.g. A biri de daing kwen a orchorn. *You are no longer a baby.*
kwen a orom unorm (n) cockerel
kwewi (adj) sharp
e.g. Idiaii nyi i kwewi.

This cutlass is sharp.
kwewikweu (adj) sharp
e.g. Chang mmi idiaii i kwewikweu. *Give me a sharp cutlass.*
kweye (v) sweep (briefly and fast)
e.g. Seng de kweye bien mbio chor. *Go and sweep away that dirt.*
kwo (prep) [se also quo] this
e.g. N kwaka kwo. *I want this.*
kwor (prep) [se also quor] that
e.g. 1. N kwaka kwor. *I want that.*
2. Unorn kwor ndior? *Is that the fowl?*
kworbere (v) relax tension (e.g. of the hand or behaviour); moderate
e.g. Kworbere kiro kingo, mbork. *Moderate your behaviour, please.*
kworkere (v) relax tension of (e.g. a rope or tie)
kworn (v) fear; escape; flee
e.g. 1. Kpara kworn. *Don't be afraid.*
2. Erequa a biri tum korm ochu quor or ka kworn. *If you don't tie that thief well he/she will escape.*

kworna (adj) small, some, a few, a little
kworni (v) fear; avoiding (adj) afraid; afraid of
e.g. 1. Or kworni mmi. *He/she fears me.*
2. Or kworni poris. *He/she is avoiding the police.*
3. Or kworni. *He/she is afraid.*
4. Or kworni rkwe. *He/she is afraid of a leopard.*
kwornorchorn (n) a young person
(adj) young
kwororo (v) to preach; to prattle
kwoya (v) scrape; scrub (briefly and fast; e.g. a finger or toe nail)
kwu (prep) this
e.g. Unorn kwu ungo? *Is this fowl yours?*

Mm

M (pro) I
e.g. M beke ning? *What did I say?*
ma (adv) that; this; here
e.g. 1. N kere ma... *I think that...*
2. Ma mmung? *What is this?*
3. Quai ma. *Come here.*
maab (v) seal (especially many holes)
maaba (adj) blocked (e.g. a hole)
e.g. Doboki dor de maaba. *That hole is blocked.*
maak (v) kick, kicked, play, played (usually football); sting (repeatedly), stung
e.g. 1. N ya u maak borl. *I like to play football.*
2. Munanong mu maak aye. *Wasps have stung him/her.*
maaka (v) plays, playing, kicking; stinging
e.g. 1. Or maaka borl. *He plays football.*
2. Be maaka borl aranghaquo. *They are playing football now.*
3. Mmung u maaka ngo nyi ndior? *What is stinging you like that?*

maan (v) kick, sting (once); open (especially an umbrella or penknife)
maba (v) cork, corked; block, blocked; push in, pushed in; seal, sealed
e.g. Or maba ekpaime chor? *Has he/she corked that bottle?*
2. Maba doboki dor a dubut. *Seal that hole in the wall.*
3. I maba doboki da ewort. *We have blocked the tunnel of a giant rat.*
mabi (v) open (especially a bottle); unseal, uncap
Maach [from Eng.] (n) March
Mai [from Eng.] (n) May
maii (v) (v) twinkle; flash (e.g. stars or lightning)
maii neen (v) blink, blinking; wink, winking; wink at (repeatdely), winking at
mak (v) mop, mop up
makara (v) wriggle; fidget; become agitated
e.g. Or makara mmung nyi ndior? *Why is he/she so agitated?*
maki (n) maggi, a soup flavouring
mama (n) mama, a child's name for mother

mamana (v) close, clench (usually a fist); press; hold firm or tight; snap (as of a trap)

mamfaibairai (n) a lie, lies
e.g. 1. Mamfaibairai! *Lies!*
2. A tangha mamfaibairai. *You are telling lies.*

mami (v) open (usually a cleched fist)
e.g. Mami ubor ungo, i ning kwa a mori. *Open your hand, let's see what you are holding.*

man (v) give birth; roll into a ball (e.g. fufu)

manana (v) to quickly roll into a ball (e.g.fufu)

manang (n) a lie; the act of spreading or making secret reports about someone or people
e.g. 1. A keri a manang ndai? *Did you think this was a lie?*
2. Onerom quor or ya kpai manang. *That man is too fond of making secret reports.*

mandai (adv) here
e.g. Quai mandai. *Come here.*

mandior (adv) there
e.g. A ka nyi mandior? *Will you go there?*

mankoro [from Eng.] (n) a mango; mangoes (fruits)

mani (v) mothered (a child), gave birth to
e.g. Meng or mani ngo? *Who gave birth to you?*
(n) a title for an elderly woman
e.g Mani Aret o quai. *Elder Aret has come.*

mansai (n) a long basket for carrying heavy load usually on the back

maruum (n) a debt; debts
e.g. N dorni u kpak maruum maimi. *I don't know how to ask for my debt.*

maya (v) twinkle, blink, wink; flash (once or momentarily)

maya...neen (v) wink at
e.g. A maya meng neen? *Who did you wink at?*

mbaini (pro) which
e.g. Ben mbaini ndai? *Which children are these?*

mbam (v) a jug
e.g. Ameme omi or chorm ikpor a mbam. *My father has a big jug.*

mbansang [from Efi.] (n) groundnut or groundnuts

mbakem (n) a short cut; an unpopular route

usually hidden from strangers or visitors

mbat [from Efi.] (n) a swamp

mbe (pro) they; them
e.g. 1. Mbe ndai. *Here they are.*
2. Bek mbe. *Tell them.*

mbebai (pro) these; these ones (usually people)

mbebor (pro) those; those ones (usually people)

mbet (n) the law; a regulation; a policy; a commandment; a taboo; contraband
e.g. 1. A chorm u kpono mbet. *You have to respect the law.*
2. Koom mbet emi. *Keep my commandement.*
3. Norborn nere a mbet. *Cartridges are contraband.*

Mbet Orbasi (n) Commandment of God

mbio (n) waste; refuse, rubbish; garbage; trash; junk; litter
e.g. N ka bieni mmang mbio chai? *Where will I dispose of this waste?*

mbiorbiort (n) water leaf, a vegetable used, usually in combination with another types of vegetable for cooking

delicious West African soup

mboon (pro) you (plural)
e.g. Mboon a? *Where are you?*

mboon na mboon (pro) amongst yourselves
e.g. U tunghi ning bu nuya mboonamboon? *How come it that you fight amongst yourselves?*

mbor (pro) it
e.g. Mbor ndai? *Is it it?*

mbork (adv) please
e.g. Mbork, kpara yain nne. *Please, don't hate me.*

mbornambor (adv) only
e.g. Buni mbornanbor? *One only?*

mborya (n) a buddy, a friend, a companion

mbuk (n) a report; news
e.g. Ta bu kpang mbuk e bangha mbe? *Have heard any news about them?*

mbuk a kpain (n) [lit. story of the past] history

mbume (n) a question
e.g. Meng o buwa mbume chor? *Who asked that question?*

mbuni (pro) which
e.g. Bunkwet mbuni ndai? *Which books are these?*

mbut! (n) an expression of non-challance meaning

"I don't care" or "Take your responsibility"

mee (v) be patient; tolerate; endure; persevere

meek (v) nod, nodded

meeke (v) tilt, tilted; bend, bent (for something to); nodding

e.g. 1. Dubut dor du meeke. *That wall has tilted.*

2. Kakam kpor ke meeke. *That plantain has bent.*

3. A biri ning arangha m meeke dono daimi? *Didn't you see how I was nodding my head?*

meekere (v) tilt (something)

e.g. A ka keme u meekere ankang a kainaii kor? *Will you be able to bend that big stick?*

meekeri (adj) not habituated; not familiar with; unfamiliar with; not fond of

e.g. 1. Ichap nyor i mekeri uka na bene. *Those animals are not yet habituated with humans.*

2. Ebia chai e mekeri na ibon. *This dog is not familar with us.*

3. M mekeri na aye. *I am not fond of him/her.*

meeki (v) choose, select

e.g. Meeki ubet a ka norngha. *Choose the room in which you will sleep.*

meen (v) swallow (e.g. eat fufu continuously); drink (habitually, e.g. beer, wine, etc)

meeng (pro) who

e.g. Meeng ndior? *Who is that?*

mek (v) choose, select

e.g. Mek kwa a ka dia. *Choose what you will eat.*

meke (v) beckon (with the hand)

e.g. Meke mmi erequa ini i kemi. *Beckon to me when it is time.*

(adj) be used to; be familiar with; become habituated

e.g. 1. N tornghor u meke na mbe. *I am beginning to be familiar with them.*

2. Ichap nyor i tornghor u meke na bene. *Those animals are beginning to be habituated with humans.*

meki (v) chose; selected; move from a leaning position

e.g. 1. Meng or meki enor chai? *Who chose this house?*

2. Kemet kor ke meki. *That fire wood has moved from its leaning position.*
meki nor (v) fall from a leaning position
e.g. Dion dor du ka meki nor, erequa a biri tum suwa ndor. *That gun will fall from its leaning position if you don't lean it well.*
men (v) swallow (fast, e.g. fufu); drink (e.g. beer, wine, etc)
miam (adj) quiet, silent
e.g. Sa miam. *Be quiet.*
mianghi (n) urine
miem (v) minimize, minimized; disrespect, disrespected; undermine, undermined
min (v) blow (usually the nose)
e.g. 1. Erequa ichon ingo I maaba min. *If your nose is blocked blow.*
2. N ka min ichon. *I will blow my nose.*
mina (v) press; switch on, e.g. a torch
mini (n) water; rain
mini mini (v) use or take by pinch; to manage by using bit by bit
(adj) watery
mkpaik (n) show-off (especially of beauty)
e.g. Ornaton quor or ya mkpaik. *That woman likes show-off.*
mkpaisin [from Efi.] (n) vaccination, inoculation
mkpork (n) slime
mkpork a korngha (n) phlegm
mkporkorbi (n) imprisonment; prison
e.g. 1. Or chorm niet dio a mkporkorbi. *He/she has ten years imprisonment.*
2. A korbor uchu a ka nyi mkporkorbi. *If you continue stealing you will go to prison.*
mkporkporor [from a masquerade that wanders about] (n) a vagabond
e.g. Kwen kwor atata mkporkporor. *That child is a typical vagabond.*
mitin [from Eng.] (n) a meeting; meetings
miiuut (n) water chevrotains
mmang (pro) where
e.g. A nyi mmang? *Where are you going?*
mmbuni (n) a lame person
mmi (pro) me
mmorng (pro) he, she; him, her

mmorng quor (pro) that; that one (usually people)
mmung (pro) what
e.g. Mmung a kwaka u sia? *What do you want to do?*
moi (v) cheat
moork (v) throw objects (especially at someone or something); harvest fruits by throwing objects at them
e.g. 1. Moork bubon bor. *Throw stones/small sticks at those goats.*
2. I kwaka u mork busokoro. *We want to pluck oranges with stones/small sticks.*
moorm (v) grope; feel someone around; search someone
e.g. 1. Kpara moorm mmi nyi ndior. *Don't search me like that.*
2. Nik u moorm mmi ini a n dat. *Stop feeling around my body when I am asleep.*
moorn (v) shoot at, throw an object at someone or something; strike at (e.g. for a snake to)
e.g. 1. Kwen quor or morn nne na unaan. *That child throw a stone at me.*
2. A duma na enu e ka moorn ngo. *If you play with a snake it will strike at you.*
moora (v) nailing, making by nailing; knocking; conking
moort (v) nail, make by nailing; knock, conk
mora (v) knock (e.g. a door); conk; hit (particularly a nail)
e.g. Mora itum a ba dion. *Knock the door before you enter.*
mork (v) be sick
e.g. Kpara mork, a kpang? *Don't be sick, OK?*
morka (v) sick; suffer from, suffering from
e.g. 1. A morka? *Are you sick?*
2. A morka mung? *What are your sick of?*
3. Or morka daak. *He/she is suffering from stammering.*
morki (adj) not sick or ill
e.g. Kating a morki? *Could it mean that you are not sick?*
mori (v) hold, holding, held; owe, owing, owed
e.g. 1. Ekpaime asik or mori. *It is not a bottle that he/she holds.*
2. A mori mmung? *What are you holding?*

3. A mori mmung aye? *What do you owe him/her?*
Mondai [from Eng.] (n) Monday
mongkwo (pro) this one e.g. Mongkwo asik. *It is not this one.*
mornghene (v) gather, assemble, unite
morni nkaim [from Eja.] (n) a young woman in a fattening room after circumcision
morni nyam [from Eja.] (n) cane rat, also known as cutting grass
mort (v) handle; hold; keep; take care of
e.g. 1. Nik or mort ukwen quor. *Let him/her handle that case.*
2. Meeng or ka mort ekpaime chai? *Who will keep this bottle?*
3. Tum mort baikait baingo. *Take good care of yourself.*
mooto [from Eng.](n) a motor, a vehicle, a car, a lorry (also used as plural)
muka (v) put into the mouth especially all the food that one is holding
muki (v) up-root (momentarily e.g. in harvesting cassava), to pull out from the roots)
mum (v) smile (continuously)
mumaa (v) hold something in the mouth or jaw
e.g. Or kemeni u tang, a ntak a o mumaa biain inwha. *He/she can't speak, because he holds something in the mouth.*
(adj) unable to speak, become dumb, especially as a result of an illness; dumbfounded, for the mouth to become shut
e.g. 1. Inwha imorng i mumaa a ntak a orkporsorng a bumork. *He has become dumb due to a serious illness.*
2. Inwha imorng i mumaa, a ntak a akpan ukwen u yarara. *He/she is dumbfounded because the truth is out.*
mumbiet (n) mongooses
mumfaikaire (n) an argument; arguments
mumi (v) smiling
e.g. A mumi mmung? *Why are you smiling?*
mumkpor (n) hawks
mumkpor ma enyam (n) monkey-eating eagles

121

muntaam (n) caps; hats
muntorere (n) explanations; narrations; statements; e.g. Be koona aye akwai a muntorere. *They call her the queen of explanations.*
mumba (n) underwears
mumbaat (n) hooves
mumbai (n) breasts; breast milk
mumbai ma eworm (n) [lit.: cow breast milk] milk
mumbe (pro) their; theirs (plurals for words beginning with "m")
e.g.1. Mumba mumbe ndai. *These are their underwears.*
2. Muntum mumbe ndai? *Are these their doors?*
mumbiet (n) mongooses
mumboot (n) wasps (those that resemble mud wasps and can also be found in a house); conks, knocks (on the head)
mumbop (n) brain; intelligence
mumbubui (n) wild pigeons
mumbubui ma orkat (n) pigeons
mundomo (n) temptations; trials
mumfaikairai (n) misunderstanding, quarrel
mumkpa (n) canes (used for beating); strokes (of the cane)
e.g. 1. Chang mmi mumkpa mor. *Give me those canes.*
2. N ka chang aye mumkpa munwan a disaing. *I will give him/her two strokes on the buttocks.*
mumkpakot (n) shoes
mumkpeke (n) curtains (used to conceal beds)
mumkpunghukpunghu (n) mumps
mun (v) is, was (sually used for nouns that begin with "min", " mun")
e.g. 1. Mini mun ka norp. *The rain will fall.*
2. Munchai mun chun aye a bakait. *He/she is short of blood.*
munai (n) insults; curses
munaii (n) money (in plural form)
e.g. N chorm munaii. *I have money/I am rich.*
munaii ma nkwet (n) pens; pencils

munanong (n) wasps (small in size and mostly in the wild)
munchab ma disaing (n) buttocks
munchabiri (n) buttocks
munchai (n) blood
munchai munkorn (v) (figuratively) have an intuition or an instinct e.g. Munhai munkorn nne. *I have an intuition/instinct.*
munchain (n) tears; cry; mourning
munchari (n) bitter kola (seeds)
mundap ma nen (n) eye lashes
munde (inf. v) is, is available; are, are available (nouns that begin with "mi" or "mu" go with "munde")
mundek (n) jaws
mundum (n) parrots
muneei (n) oil
muneei ma ekeng (n) python oil
muneei ma mfor (n) njabe oil
muneei ma soi (n) honey
muneei ma inoi (n) poga oil
muneei ma bukorma (n) rubbing oil
muneei mundoni (n) red palm oil
munen (n) blue duikers (a specified and an unspecified number of)
munfiaim (n) whistles (made of metal or plastic)
munfum (n) stools (especially for the kitchen)
munkakani (n) fishing cage-traps made of bamboos (a specified and an unspecified number of)
munken (n) tilapias
munkene (n) cockroaches
munkoko (n) feathers
munkom (n) njasasnga", "njansang", seeds used for thickening and flavouring soup
munkooma (n) gizzards
munkorng (n) perewinkles
munkormor (n) drums
munkot (n) spoons
munkot ma nenen (n) forks
munkpai (n) the two divided parts or lips (especially of virgina)
munkpainyin (n) scorpions
munkpakot (n) shoes

munkpe (n) cases, court cases; judgments
munkpeke (n) curtains (used to conceal beds)
munku (n) bay duikers
munkung (n) chests
munkuuka (n) wounds
munkuyoork (n) otters
munkwou (n) hunger
munok (n) drink (whiskey, beer, or wine)
munork (n) salt
munorng (n) wood ash
munornoi (n) fingers
munsat (n) nets (especially the type put across a river)
munsop (n) fines
munsung (n) messengers
munsosoka (n) weaver birds
muntai (n) calves (of the legs)
muntaim (n) pieces of advice; counsels; recommendations; proposals; suggestions
muntam (n) caps; hats
muntem (n) a string of beads, usually worn roung the neck or waist
muntork (n) sand flies
muntort (n) birds
muntort ma ekai (n) palm birds
muntort ma orkat (n) cattle egrets
munchari (n) bitter kola (plural with no specific number)
muntorere (v) narration, narrations; statement, statements
e.g. Ba muntorere mumorng. *Take his/her statement.*
muntuum [from Efi.] (n) doors
munwain (n) shins
munwakara (n) junctions, bifurcations; confluences,
munwha (n) mouths; squirrels
munwha ma mumbai (n) nipples
munyangha (n) palm kernel oil
munyai nyaii (n) bush pigs, red river hogs
munyai nyaii ma orkat (n) pigs (domestic)
munyononi (n) stars; whistles (made through the mouth)
muuk (v) devour, put a lot of food into the mouth at a time before chewing
muuki (v) up-root continuously (e.g. in

harvesting cassava), to pull out from the roots
muum (v) grumble, complain; hum
muuma (v) smile (briefly)
muuntaam (n) caps; hats
muuntuum (n) doors (a specified and an unspecified number of)

Nn

i (pro) we, it
na (conj) and, with, together with; through
e.g. 1. Ngo na mmi biain buni. [lit.: *You and me are one thing*] *We are relatives.*
2. N ka numa ngo inaii nyor na aye. *I shall send you that money through him.*
(inf.v) has not, have not
e.g. Or na quai. *He/she has not come.*
naan (n) medicines; drugs
naan na dayawa (n) love charms
naaraan (n) monitor lizards
naba (adj) scarce
e.g. Ichap i naba ndurie. *Meat is/animals are scarce nowadays.*
na daikwai (adv) in the day, by day
e.g. N ya dusend na daikwai. *I like travelling by day.*
na dei (adv) at night, by night
e.g. 1. Or quai na dei. *He/she came at night.*
2. N yani u seng da dei. *I don't like travelling by night.*

nafia (n) slaps
nai (v) to insult (repeatedly)
naifaibairai (n) sparrows
naifaikayo (n) umbrellas
naik (v) sharpen
e.g. Naik idiaii nyor. *Sharpen that cutlass.*
naikain (n) tails
naim (v) shine; glow; reflect
naimi (v) shining; glowing; reflecting
naina (v) mention; put a tapping container in place to collect the liquid
e.g. 1. Kpara naina din dimi. *Don't mention my name*
2. Naina desip a orkem quor. *Put a calabash under the palm (to collect the wine)*
naip (v) direct (especially someone where to find something)
e.g. Naip nne eyain a koomi edising chor. *Direct me where you have kept that knife*
nairaii (n) oil palms
nairaii na orkat (n) [lit.: whiteman's palms]pineapples
nairon (n) nylon

nairuk (adj) another, other, some other (for nouns beginning with "ne", "na", "nor" or "no"
e.g. 1. Neyen nairuk nere? *Are there other plums?*
2. Nasan nairuk ndai. *Here are some other plates.*
naisairai (n) Sunbirds
e.g. Naisaisai ne ya echimini chai. *Sunbirds like these fruits.*
naisip (n) calabashes (many and also a specifiued number of)
naiyin (n) families
na kabat (adv) in the afternoon, at noon
nakan (n) messages
nakaara (n) curtains (especially of Ekwe or grand, public ocassions)
nakat (n) whitemen
na kito (adv) in the morning
na kori (adv) in the evening; at dusk
nakwau (n) ampits
nami (v) take (as an encouragement by an onlooker)); seize
nan (adj) be fortunate; be blessed; be free
e.g. 1. N nan. *I am fortunate/blessed*
2. N nan aye a ubor. *I am free from his/her hand.*
nanaan (n) stones; cartridges; (a euphemism) batteries
nanani (n) wounds; injuries
nanau (n) thighs
nang (v) spread secret information about someone; make or give out a secret report about someone
e.g. Or nang nne. *He has made a secret report against me.*
nani (v) straighten, iron
nani iworn [lit.: straighten feet](v) stroll (a euphemistic expression)
nanwa (n) cats (pussy cats)
nanyeng (n) absesses
nap (adj) scarce
e.g. Ichap i tornghor u nap urum ubon. *Animals are beginning to be scarce in our forest.*
nadaikang [from Efi](n) matches; match boxes
nasaam (n) spears (a specified and an unspecified number of)
nasan (n) plates; bowls (a specified and an unspecified number of)

nasona pak [from Eng.](n) National Park

nau (v) scratch (continuously especially to reduce itching)

nawa (v) scratch (briefly especially to reduce itching)

nawam (n) hooks

nawan (n) a canoes

nawan na inchin (n) (lit: engine canoes) engine boats; speed boats

nawoo! (inj) an expression of disappointment or bitter surprise

naya (v) insult, abuse (once or for a moment)

na a yaya na a yani (conj) like it or not

e.g. Na a yaya na a yani, n ka quai a enor engo ndaikwai. *Like it or not, I shall come to your house today.*

nchaini (pro) which (for nouns beginning with "n"

e.g. A ya nkwet nchaini? *Which book do you like?*

ncheneruk (adv) perhaps, perchance, maybe, possibly

e.g. 1. Ncheneruk or ka quai? *Perhaps he/she will come.*

nchornanchor (adv) only

e.g. Chaini nchornanchor. *One only.*

ndai (adv) here; this is/these are, is this/are these; this, these

e.g. 1. Mmi ndai. *Here I am.*
2. Chaap ndai. *This is an animal/This is meat.*
3. Mmung ndai? *What is this?*

ndaikwai (adv) today; tonight

ndaing (adv) here; this way

ndaini (pro) which

e.g. Dorkorng ndaini ndai? *Which pot is this?*

ndek (n) dirt, filth

ndere (conj) because

e.g. Kating ndere a tunghi esaing a enor inyene? *Is it because you come from wealthy familiy?*

ndior (adv) abosultely, exactly; right, that's right

e.g. Ndior. *Absolutely/right/that's right.*

ndior asik (v) isn't it

e.g. 1. Dusarari du nyangha u sai Kororp ke re dorbork dorbork, ndior asik? *Disunity has contributed to making Kororp remain backward, isn't it?*

ndiro (n) a mouth organ
ndisime [from Efi.] (n) rubbish; stupidity
ndor (adv) there
ndorng (n) group, team; line, file
e.g. 1. Or reni a ndorng aibon. *He is not in our team.*
2. Baat a ndorng. *Stand in a line.*
3. Nik i send a ndorng chaini. *Let's move in a single file.*
ndornandor (adv) only
e.g. Duni ndornandor. *One only.*
nduk (n) soup (from pottage food)
ndukndian [from Efi.](n) pen-knife
nduni (pro) which
Duchai nduni ndai? *Which stream is this?*
ndurie (adv) these days, nowadays; present generation
e.g. 1. N dorni utibe na aye ndurie. *I don't know what is wrong with him nowadays.*
2. Ben ba ndurie be kpononi bene. *Children of the present generation don't respect people.*
ne (art.) are; has; have

e.g. Rairaii ne re. *There are palm nuts.*
(v) meet, accost
e.g. Ne aye. *Meet him/her.*
nebereng (n) valleys
e.g. Nebereng ne chawi kpai katana kai. *There are too many valleys in this area.*
neeke (n) stories, tales; histories
neeke na kpain (n) [lit. Stories of the past] folklore
neen (n) eyes
neep (v) to litter (with dirt), to dirty
neeyeen (n) plums (a specified or unspecified number of)
neeyeen na orkat (n) pears or alvocados
neh (v) clear (e.g. grass or farm), cut (e.g. grass); meet
e.g. 1. Neh karam. *Clear the grass.*
2. Neh nsangha emi. *Meet my friend.*
nekang (n) saltlick
e.g. Ichaap i quai a nekang nai a kporkporor ini. *Animals visit this slatlick regularly.*
neke (adj) tasty, palatable
e.g. Borkor bor be neke? *Is that food tasty/palatable?*

neke neke (adj) tasty, palatable
e.g. N ya borkor be neke neke. *I like tasty food*
nekebe (n) boxes; coffins
nekem (n) felled oil palms, for tapping
nekere (adv) well; thoroughly, properly; really, actually; diligently, skillfully; well; studiuosly
e.g. 1. Nekere kpang a ba buk. *Hear well before you report.*
2. Nekere kwop mbe. *Beat them thoroughly.*
3. Onaton quor or nekere normi. *That woman is really beautiful.*
4. Nekere sai duwom dungo. *Do your work diligently.*
5. Or nekere yait nkwet chai. *He/she has written this book skillfully.*
6. A nekere yeu udomo ungo? *Have you passed your exams well?*
7. Or nekere kpaka kakpat kemorng enain ko kwen quor or nor. *He/she studiously blocked the way with his foot so that the child should fall.*
nekeri (adv) does not really
e.g. Or nekeri dor kikaim ki. *He/she does not really know this area.*
nekesu (n) small cages (like the fishing type) for trapping rats; a euphemism for cage-traps for fishing
nem (n) crack (especially kernel)
e.g. Nyangha ornwa u nem ichu. *Help your mother crack palm kernels.*
neme (v) discuss, converse; dialogue
nem (v) cracking
e.g. A nemi mmung? *What are you cracking?*
nenene (v) meet up with; encounter
nendindi (n) lizards (the small, dark type)
nere (v) cussion with; pad with.
e.g. Nere ikwang ekpa chor a ba koorn bukpait bor. *Pad the bag with leaves before you put the cocoyams.*
neruk (adj) another (for words that begin with "na", "ne")
e.g. 1. Nasan neruk. *Another plates/bowls.*
2. Or chormi norkorng neruk. *He/she doesn't have another pots.*

3. N chorm nororibot neruk. *I have another pillows.*

neu (adj) cold; be silent, calm (to be)
e.g. 1. Mini bu neu ! *The water, so cold!*
2. Neu! *Be silent!*

neuwi (adj) cold; silent; quiet
e.g. 1. Or ya mini mu neuwi. *He/she likes cold water.*
2. Urumanyen u neuwi saaii. *The (virgin) forest is eerie silent.*

neuwineu (adj) cold; quiet; silent
e.g.1. N ya mini mu neuwineu. *I like cold water.*
2. Ayain chai e neuwineu nning ndai? *Why is this place so quiet?*

newe (v) nullify (especially a charm); neutralize (especially a poison)

newere (v) make a hot thing cold by pouring or addition cold water; cool down oneself, for instance, with a cold drink or a cold shower

nfina [from Efi.](n) trouble, problem; misunderstanding

nfor (n) a tree, commonly called njabe, whose seeds are used to produce edible oil and whose chaff can be used to poison fish as a method of fishing; seeds of the tree

nforokum [from Efi.] (n) cotton; [euphemism] light
e.g. Eta emi ere nforokum. *My clothes is cotton.*

nfuk (n) dust

ngha (adj) like, as, such as
e.g. 1. N kwaka afarawa quo or normi ngha eyo. *I want a flower that is beautiful like the setting sun.*
2. N kwaka orne quo or fara kenweye, ngha Akparika. *I want someone that runs fast, such as Akparika.*

ngharangha (adv) the way; as; as much as, as well as
e.g. 1 Bebe ngharangha m bebe. *Jump the way I jumped*
2. Sai ngharangha m beke ngo. *Do as I told you.*
3. Ekese a bene be yani aye ngharangha be ya Ojom. *Many people don't*

like him as much as they like Ojom.
4. Be kemeni u sai duwom du ngharangha ibom i sai. *They cannot do this job as well as we do.*
nghie (v) excrete; lay (usually an egg)
nghwam (v) carry, transport, convey
ngo (pro) you (singular)
ngo kating (pro) alone, solo
e.g. A ka keme u seeng ngo kating? *Will you be able to travel solo?*
ngweek (v) fetch, fetched (e.g. by splitting or cutting fire wood)
ngweeke (v) break, broken (for something to do so on its own)
ngween (v) break (especially a stick)
e.g. A keme u ngween kainaii kor? *Can you break that stick?*
ngweep (v) dig
ngweke (v) press; press down
e.g. Kainaii ke ngweke uworn umorng. *A stick has pressed his/her foot.*
ngwei (v) run; escape
ngwei kworn (v) escape

e.g. Onerom quo or ka ngwei kworn. *This man will escape.*
ngwep (v) fan
e.g. Ngwep mmi. *Fan me.*
nghwet (v) thrust the waist forward and backward; rotake the hip
ngwornghor (v) swear; take an oath
e.g. A keme u nwornghor? *Can you swear?*
ngweye (v) run; escape
ngwingha (v) hint
e.g. Ngwingha mmi erequa a kpanghi a be tornghor u quai. *Hint me when you hear they have started coming.*
nh (v) take (an informal expression, pronounced with the mouth shut)
ni (adv) there
e.g. Nion ni re. *There are guns.*
nichaii (n) streams (a specified number of)
niet (n) years
niimi (v) sweat, perspire
niin (n) names
nik (v) leave someone alone; stop doing something; let something be; let

niki (v) climb (especially steps, bed, chair and other small heights)
nin (n) hair
ninini (v) argue; contend with; debate
e.g. 1. Kpara ninini. *Don't argue.*
2. Or ya u ninini na ibon. *He/she is fond of debating with us.*
ning (v) see, saw, seen; find, found; witness, witnessed; experience, experienced
ninghi (v) recognize, make out; don't…see; don't/can't see; don't/can't see find
e.g. 1. A keme u ninghi aye? *Can you recognize him/her?*
2. Be ninghi kwa a n sai ma. *They recognize what I do here.*
3. A ninghi arang or dunghi na ibon? *Don't you see how he lives with us?*
4. Be ninghi ibon ma. *They do not see us here.*
5. Nke echor a ninghi daing a urum umbe. *You can't find even a snail in their forest again.*
niorn (n) grey hair
e.g. N tornghor u chorma niorn. *I have started having grey hair.*
nirorp (n) languages (a specified number of)
e.g. N keme utang nirorp ninai. *I can speak four languages.*
nisuwi (n) veins (a specified number of)
niyik (n) horns (a specified number of)
e.g. Enoom e chorm niyik niwan. *A red duiker has two horns.*
nkaim (n) circumcision; a period of seclusion after circumcision
nkan (n) a joke
nkakebaare (n) a misfortune; an agent of misfortune; a demon; a curse, a spell
nkari (n) a trick, cunning, con
e.g. Or kemeni u dummmi nkari. *He/she cannot play me a trick.*
nkarika [from Efi.](n) a bell; a clock; time
nkarika a ubor (n) a wrist watch
nkat (n) show-off (especially of beauty)
nke (conj) even; not even; no matter; although; even though, albeit

e.g. 1. Nke morng or chee ngo. *Even he/her gossips about you.*
2. Nke chaap chaini? *Not even one animal?*
3. Nke mmung, n ka yeu uromo umi. *No matter what, I will pass my exams.*

nke kwanaka (adv) even a little; at all

e.g. Chang mm inke kwanaka. *Give me even a little.*
2. N dorni aye nke kwanaka. *I don't know him/her at all.*

nkendior (conj) even so, that notwithstanding, nevertheless, nonetheless, however

Nkondup (n) an extinct village of Kororp, some members of which have been assimilated into Ekon

nkoorn (n) a joint

nkornankor (adv) only

e.g. Kaini nkornankor. *One only.*

nkpaik (n) a display; show-off, especially of beauty or some other special qualities

nkpaisin [from Efi.] (n) vaccination

e.g. Kwen ongo o nuwa nkpaisin? *Has your child taken vaccination?*

nkpaka (n) a button

nkpanyan (n) a ring

nkpanyan a dunung (n) ear ring

nkpanyan a ubor (n) finger ring

nkui (n) maize (singular or plural)

nkumanang (n) bahama grass

nkwet [from Efi.] (n) book; letter; schooling; learning; academics, education

e.g. 1. N chorm ikpor a nkwet. *I have a big book.*
2. Mbork, de yait chang mmi nkwet. *Please, come and help me write a letter.*
3. Kwen quo or na tornghor nkwet. *This child has not started schooling.*
4. Nkwet e re eti a biain. *Education is a good thing.*

nkwet a dono (n) [lit.: book of the head] an identity card; a passport

Nkwet Orbasi (n) [lit.: book of God] the Bible; the Koran, etc.

nkwoni (conj) which

nkwor u sai (conj) the reason why

nna (conj) and; with; together with

nnaini (pro) which
e.g. Nono nnaini ndai? *Which heads are these?*

nnangha (conj) but; but then; and then? so what?
e.g. 1. N kere u fuum aye, nnangha amene ormorng o dion quai. *I thought of beating him, but his father entered.*
2. Nnangha? A ka sai mmung? *So what? What will you do?*

nndiise (n) a show; a spectacle; a display; an exhibition

nne (pro) me
e.g. Ekese a bene ma be ya nne. *Many people here love me.*

Nnee (n) [Dukonokondo] Mama, Mother

nneme (n) a discussion, a conversation; dialogue
e.g. 1. N ka yau u chorma nneme na ngo. *I will like to have a discussion with you.*
2. Dion na mbe a nneme. *Enter into dialogue with them.*

nning (adv) what
e.g. U bura nning? *What does it mean?*

nnor (pro) you (special usage in plural)
e.g. 1. Quai nnor. *Come on you.*
2. Mmung, nnor? *What, you?*
3. Bari nnor. *Get out you.*

nnyini (pro) which

nobo (n) kolanuts (a specified and an unspecified number of)

nokot (n) shadows; silhouettes

nokpokentei (n) termite mounds (see okpokentei)

nokui (n) electric fish (plural)

nokumambok (n) woodpeckers

nokun (n) ralatives, family members – brothers, sisters, cousins, aunts, uncles
e.g. Nokun naimi ndai. *These are my relatives.*

nokpokoro (n) tables
e.g. A chorm nokpokoro nawang. *How many tables do you have?*

nono (n) heads (a specified and an unspecified number of)

nontoninkang (n) lamps

nookon (n) farms

nookot (n) inlaws

nookpo (n) corpses (see ookpo)
noorba (v) submerge; plunge
noorkor (n) wealth, property (plural)
noormi (adj) not beautiful, not nice; not fair, not good; not advisable
e.g. U noormi u nwei na dei. *It is not advisable to run in the night.*
nor (v) strike (e.g. thunder); fall
e.g. 1. Erequa duwewei du yewe, dor a duwam du ka nor. *If the lightning passes, know that thunder will strike.*
2. A yonini kpai a ka nor. *If you spin round too much you will fall.*
(pro) [implied] everyone
e.g. Quai nor. *Come everyone.*
norba (v) raining; soak
e.g. 1. Mini mu norba. *The rain is falling.*
2. Mu norba aranghaquo. *It is raining now.*
2. Norba ita ingo. *Soak your clothes.*
norborn (n) cartridges; bullets
nor chaap (v) to convulse; convulsed

Norfemba [from Eng.] (n) November
nori [Duk.] (v) touch (usually lightly)
norkorkoi (n) kingfishers
norngkorng (n) song birds
norkpor (n) rubber; plastic (plural); rubber trees
norkporkoror (n) nucturnal spirit-masquarades in Kororp known more for their entertaining songs
norkwork (n) graters
norkworkirinua [from Efi.](n) handkerchiefs
norm (v) be good; be beautiful
norma (v) cause someone to bear the cause of a mishap, make someone bear a responsibility for which one is not prepared; add to one's responsibility, burden
normi (adj) beautiful, nice; fair, good; advisable
norn (v) go to the farm or "bush"
norngha (n) [lit.: Sleep] good night
e.g. 1. Norngha. *Good night.*
(v) lie (down), sleep; sleep with, have sex with; share a bed with

1. Work kwen quor ko or daat. *Dandle that child so he/she can sleep.*
2. U noormi u norngha na ominkei. *It is not good to have sex with a relative.*
3. N yani u norngha na orne a korchoorn. *I don't like to share a bed with a snoring person.*

nornghene (v) place; lay
e.g. 1. Nornghene inaii nyor ma. *Place that money here.*
2. Nornghene kwen quor a bekork baimi. *Lay that child on my bed.*

nornor (n) toes
nornorn (n) chickens
nornorn na orkat (n) ducks
nornyorm (n) bush mango fruits or trees (a specified number of)
nornwhororor (n) toads
norom (n) knees
nororibot [from Efi.](n) pillows
norp (v) rain
e.g. Mu nka norp ndaikwai. *It will rain today.*
nors [from Eng.] (n) a nurse
nortor (n) songs
nortorp (n) mud (plural)

nortorp nortorp (adj) muddy; marshy, swampy
notoninkang [from Efi.](n) lamps
nquni (pro) which
e.g. Uworn nquni u nuu ngo? *Which leg pains you?*
nquornanquor (adv) only
e.g. Kwoni nquornanquor. *One only.*
nsai (n) an idea; a thought; an opinion
nsangha [from Efi.] (n) a friend
nsep (n) an illness believed to be due to a poison or charm
nset (n) a plain, a level land
nsibidi (n) a traditional society in Kororp that represents the military
nsome (n) trouble; nuisance
(e.g. Kwen quor or kwaka nsome. *That child is looking for trouble.*
(adj) troublesome
e.g. Kwen quor or re orne a nsome. *That child is a troublesome person.*
nsop (n) a levy, a contribution, a subscription
nsork (n) instigation
nsu (n) a lie; fake

e.g. 1. Or ya u tang nsu. *He/she fond of telling lies.*
2. Imum nyor i re nsu. *That smile is fake.*
(adj) false
e.g. Tina "akpanukwen" bor "nsu". *Tick "true" or "false".*
nsuk ikang [from Efi.] (n) a ship
nta (n) times; multipled by
e.g. 1. Nta orwang? *How many times?*
2. Buwan nta dio. *Two multipled by ten.*
ntak (n) purpose, objective, aim; reason, rationale; sake
e.g. 1. Ntak a kwoba aye a? *Why did you beat him/her?*
2. Ntak a kochuka kai e re ko i chorma ini u chang bantem itaim. *The reason for this gathering is so that we have the opportunity to adivse one another.*
3. N quai ma a ntak engo. *I have come here for your sake.*
ntak a (pro) why
ntebesi (adj) upside down
ntem [also Eja.]((n) a friend; a companion, a colleague; a counterpart
ntem ekan (n) age-mate

ntoofuk (n) a fishing net (that is cast to catch fish)
e.g. Ndorni u moork ntoofuk. *I don't knoxw how to cast a fishing net.*
ntume (n) confusion
e.g. Kpara a baquai ntume ma. *Don't bring confusion here.*
ntume ntume (adv) carelessly; confusedly
nu (v) fight; weave especially a basket; ache, pain
e.g. 1. Kpara nu. *Don't fight.*
2. A dor u nu kobom? *Do you know how to weave a basket?*
3. Dorom de nu nne. *My knee aches.*
nuka (v) have sex (especially animals); set (quickly, especially a trap)
e.g. Nuka keeteei mandior. *Set a trap there.*
nukere (v) bend; bow
e.g. 1. Nukere kainai kor. *Bend that stick.*
2. Nukere dono daingo. *Bow your head.*
nuuk (v) set (especially many traps)
nuuka (v) bow down; dock

nuuka ket (v) [lit.: bend down and look] think carefully, look into, consider

num (v) send (someone on an errand)

e.g. Num aye. *Send him/her.*

num be kona (v) send for

e.g. Num be kona aye. *Send for him/her.*

numa (v) send (something to someone)

e.g. Numa mmi eti a biain. *Send me something nice.*

numene (v) try; test, tempt; try on (e.g. clothes)

e.g. 1. N ka numene u nwam donuna dai kating. *I will try to carry this luggage alone.*

2. Numene aye. *Test him/her.*

3. Numene eta chor aba deu nchor. *Try on the clothes before you buy it.*

4. Kpara numene mmi, ngo setan quo. *Don't tempt me, you this satan.*

numene iromo (v) tempt, put to a test

e.g. N ka numene aye iromo ko n dor bor ore eti a kwen. *I will put him/her to test so I know whether he/she is a good child.*

numm (v) grow; grow up; develop; mature

nun (v) glance at, glancing at; regard, view, admire

e.g. 1. Or ya u nun mmi. *He/she is fond of glancing at me.*

2. Nun baikait a okutiso. *Admire yourself in the mirror.*

nuna (v) hurt a wound (by adding pressure on it); thread (usually a needle), thread something using a bamboo or string

nuu (v) anahilate, deciminate

nuumene (v) take measurements of; measure to determine the quantity of

nuun (v) thread using bamboos or string

nuuna (v) lift up especially a load unto one's head

nuuna nuuna (v) carry on the head

nuwa (v) pierce; inject

e.g. 1. Kaikwai ke nuwa kakpaat kaimi. *A thorn has pierced my foot.*

2. Or kwaka u nuwa mi abiabun. *He/she wants to give me an injection.*

nuya (v) fight in a group
e.g. Bayo bai be ya u nuya. *These people like to fight.*
nwak (v) eat fast, devour
e.g. Or ya u nwak daria ngha ebia. *He is fond of devouring food like a dog.*
nwham (v) carry; help, support, facilitate
nwindo (n) a window
nwingha (v) hint
nyai (v) hurt, pain
e.g Kpara mamana kpai, u nyai. *Don't press too much, it hurts.*
nyam (v) sell; (figuratively) betray
e.g. 1. Or kwaka u nyam ekpang chai. *He/she wants to sell this farm.*
2. Ntangha chang ngo u tibe aranghaquo, nnangha kpara nyam nne. *I am telling you what is happening now, but don't betray me.*
nyangha (v) help; facilitate; assist
e.g. 1. Mbork, quai de nyangha mmi. *Please, come and help me.*
2. Munaii mu mu nka nyangha duwom dumi. *This money will facilitate my work.*

nye (v) excrete, excreting, excreted, pass out, passing out, passed out
nyenghe (adj) sweet
e.g Suka or ngyenghe. *Sugar is sweet.*
nyenghe nyenghe (adj) sweet
e.g. N ya orkem or ngyengh engyenghe. *I like sweet palm wine.*
nyenghene (v) sweeten
nyenene (adv) again
nyenyenghe (n) Indian bamboo
nyi (adv) this; like
 e.g. 1. Idiaii nyi *This cutlass.*
2. Sai nyi ndai. *Do it like this.*
3. Ini nyi a n tangha ta i quai. *The time that I talk about has come.*
(v) go; to bury
e.g. 1. A kwaka u nyi mmang? *Where do you want to go?*
2. Ta be nyi ebia chor ekwa? *Have they buried the dog that just died?*
nyi ndai (adv) Like this; in this manner
e.g. 1. Seng nyi ndai. *Walk like this.*
nyi ndior (adv) Like that; Amen

140

e.g. 1. Mmung u choki nyi ndior? *What is shouting like that?*
2. Orbasi o tooni ngo. Nyo ndior. *God bless you. Amen.*

nyiort (v) massage

nyoorni (v) become slippery

e.g. Ainain chai e tornghor u nyoorni. *This road has started becoming slippery.*

nyornanyor (adv) only

e.g. Nyini nyornanyor. *One only.*

nyornini (adj) slippery

e.g. Ainain chai e nyornini kpai. *This road is too slippery.*

nyoori (v) iron; massage (repeatedly)

nyori (v) iron; massage (quickly)

e.g. 1. Nyori nne eta chai. *Iron this clothes for me.*
2. Nyori baikait baimi. *Massage my body.*

nyuuk (v) maltreat

e.g. U noormi u nyuuk bantem. *It is not good to maltreat others.*

Oo

o (v) he/she is, he/she has
e.g. 1. O quai. *He/she is coming.*
2. O kaik. *He/she has gone.*
obaii a durau (n) a nightmare
obaii a esin (n) bad heartedness
obon (pro) our; ours
e.g. Okuma obon ndai. *This is our last lastborn.*
obufa [from Efi.] ((adj) new, strange
e.g. Mmung u re obufa mandior? *What is new there?*
Obufa a Diet (n) New Year
ochu (n) a thief
oduki (n) [see also oruki] a cruel, evil, wicked or dangerous person; a villain; a criminal
ofebere (n) a sparrow
ofiri (adj) whole
e.g. 1. Ofiri ini nyi a sai mmung? *What have you done this whole time?*
2. N kwaka ekwem chor ofiri. *I want that fish whole.*
oforng irem [from Efi.] (n) shirt
ofufuk (n) midges
ofufung (n) wind
ofura (n) indigestion
e.g. Kwen quo or chorm ofur a. *This child has indigestion.*
Ojom (n) a Kororp male name
Ojong [from Eja.] (n) a Kororp male name
okaisu (n) a small cage for trapping rats (like the cage trap for fishing); a euphemism for cage trap for fishing
okirika (n) secondhand clothes
okongha (n) a chameleon
okoroni (n) a golden barb (fish), about or a little smaller that "chorng"
Okoryorng (n) a one time clan of Kororp, split from Kororp by war, now an ethnic group in Odukpani Local Government Area of the Cross River State of Nigeria, now reconnected to the rest of Kororp
okpiya (n) an orphan
okpokentei (n) a termite mound that looks like a wild mushroom; using the termite mound, it is a juju that is believed to

cause someone's body to swell badly.

okpo (n) a small bag used by a hunter to carry cartridges and other such hunting gear.

okpokoro [from Efi.] (n) a table

okpoo (n) a non-initiate (especially of a society)

okpuk (n) a high fever (especially that which causes the body to shiver or tremble)

e.g. Okpuk o kuba mmi. *I have a high fever.*

okukup (n) a cover (especially of a container such as a pot)

okum (n) a market; a week; price, cost

okuma (n) lastborn

okumambok (n) a woodpecker

okumankpa (n) a spider

okumi (n) a large needle made from an umbrella spoke and used for sewing bags, etc

okut a ekwe (n) a rank in ekwe

okut iso [from Efi.] (n) mirror

okwakwai (n) an impotent man

okwom (n) a barren person (especially a woman)

Omuna (n) Lord

ondindi (n) a lizard (the small, black type)

ononoki (n) a drunkard; a dipsomaniac

onum (adj) old

e.g. Onum eta. *Old clothes.*

Onum a Diet (n) [lit.: Old year] Christmas

oo (adj) OK; yes

ookpo (n) a corpse; a diaphragm

oorborn (n) a cartridge; a bullet

oorkpak (n) a poor person

oorngwa (n) mother, usually meaning 'your mother'

e.g.Chaina ornwa. *Greet your mother.*

oorsaam (n) a living room, a parlour; a hall

oorsaam ekwe (n) an Ekpe hall, a hall of the highest traditional society that is also used by other traditional societies

oorsere (n) oversea, abroad, foreign land or country

e.g. 1. Kwen ormorng or re oorsere. *His/her child is overseas.*

2. Kwen omi o nyi oorsere. *My child has gone abroad.*
onum (adj) old; experienced
e.g. 1. Onum ekpa ndai. *This is an old bag.*
2. N de onum orne a kana kai. *I am an experienced person in this subject (branch of study).*
onwingnwing (n) mosquitoes
onyin (n) gums (of the teeth)
or (pro) he, she
e.g. 1. Or reni ma. *He/she is not here.*
2. Or na quai. *He/she has not come yet.*
3. Or ri quai. *He/she will not come.*
(v) he/she is; he/she has
e.g. Or quai. *He/she is coming.*
2. Or quai. *He has come.*
orairio [from Eng.](n) radio
or ba (conj) then; before
e.g. 1. N dion, or ba tung qai. *I entered, then he/she appeared.*
2. Ta i tornghor u dia biain be ba dion. *We had started eating before they entered.*
orbang (n) Harmattan

Orbasi (n) God
orbei (n) foolishness; imbecility
orbereng (n) a valley
orbian (n) a lazy person
e.g. A re orbian. *You are a lazy person.*
orborn (n) a chief, a king; a traditional dance society
orborom (n) right hand (adj) right side
orboror (n) a medium-size drum
orbereng (n) a valley
orchorka (n) destruction, devastation; rampage
e.g. 1. I na ning utor a quo orchroka mandai. *We have not witnessed this kind of devastation here.*
2. Bai dion orchorka. *They have gone on a rampage.*
orfa (n) luck; fortune
orfanganfoot (n) a grasshopper
orfat (n) a twin
orforng irem [from Efi.] (n) a shirt
oriornghor [from Efi.] (n) a male or female friend with whom one shares sexual relationship
orip (n) a rainy day or period (when rain falls continually for a whole day or for several days)

orka (n) a craftsman; an artist
orkani (n) a ghost; an aparition
orkat (n) a whiteman
orkebe (n) a box; a coffin
orkem (n) palm wine (from oil palm)
orken (n) a stranger; a visitor
orkenenken (n) a butterfly
orkesu (n) (n) small cages (like the fishing type) for trapping rats; a euphemism for cage-traps for fishing
orkorkatai (n) a long, edible fruit with a number of fleshy seeds, popularly called monkey kola
orkorkoi (n) a kingfisher; (figuratively) a skilled fisherman
orkorng (n) a song bird
Orkorst [from Eng.] (n) August
orkpa (n) river, a Durorp name for an Ejagham or a Banyangi person
orkpaan (n) a selfish person
orkpa a fururu (n) a lake
Orkpa Ina (n) the largest of Kororp rivers, between Erat and Ekornganaku
orkpakara [from Efi.] (n) a table chair
Orkpasang (n) known officially as Akpasang, a Kororp river on the bank of which lies the village of Orkpasang whose name is derived from the river
Orkporkobait (n) an extinct village of Kororp, some members of which have been assimilated into Ekornganaku
orkpor (n) rubber; plastic; a rubber tree
orkporor (v) a harlot
orkporsorng [from Efi.] (adv) firmly; seriously (adj) serious; great
orkwork (n) a grater
ormanini (n) a nursing mother, a birth-giving woman
ormankor (n) a sugar cane
ormorn (n) a lion
ormormorki (n) a sickling e.g. Kwen kwo or de atata ormormorki. *This child is a typical sickling.*
ormkpiik (n) a flying fox
ornananghi (n) a liar; a person who spreads secret information or

makes secret reports about people
ornanari (adj) mad (n) a mad person
ornaton (n) a woman
orne (n) a human, a person; someone
orne a kanaat (n) a mad person
orne a Aboong (n) a person of Abung
orne a Ekorn (n) a person of Ekorn
orne a Ekornganaku (n) a person of Ekornganaku
orne a Erat (n) a person of Erat
orne a Nkondup (n) a person of Nkondup
orne a Ngworo (n) a person of
orne a Orkpokobait (n) a person of Orkpokobait
orne a Orkoryorng (n) a person of Orkoryorng
orne ambunghor (n) a lame person
orne amoi (n) a cheat
orne a nsu (n) a liar
orne a enork (n) a soldier
ornenum (adj) elderly (n) an elder, an elderly person
orne a inung (n) a deaf person

orne a ita (n) a law enforcement officer
orne oruk (n) someone else
ornerom (n) a man
orne a ukut (n) an marginalised; a disadvantaged; an underprivileged; a deprived; a needy person
ornkenenken (n) a butterfly
ornorm (n) a beauty, a belle
ornornormi (n) a dancer
ornworngwornghor (n) a string of beads made of metal, usually but not always mixed with small bells, worn by a woman in a traditional "school" such as fattening room after circumcision
ornwororor (n) a toad
orom (n) a husband
orom a buqun (n) hernia, appendicitis
Ororp (n) a Kororp person
orsorsoi (n) small snails that often destroy the vegetative parts of crops
orworna (n) tobacco; snuff (i.e. tobacco powder)

orteke (n) a verandah
ortor (n) a singer
oruk (adj) another (for words that begin with "o")
e.g. Orne oruk. *Another person.*
oruki (n) [see also oduki] a cruel, evil, wicked or dangerous person; a villain; criminal
orsa (n) a witch or wizard
orsaam (n) a spear
orsengheene (n) maltreatment, mistreatment, abuse
osare (n) fibre made from a plantain or a banana stem
osairai (n) a Sunbird
osi (n) measles
osit (n) a babysitter
otibi (n) okra
otiri (n) thigh pains due to strenuous trekking
Otoba [from Eng.] (n) October
otoko (n) pepper
otou ese (n) bitterleaf
owowomi (n) a hard-working person
oyim (n) onions (in general)
oyim urum (n) wild onion (a fruit) popularly known as "country" onion
oyim orkat (n) onions (a bulb, commonly sold in the market)

Pp

"P" does not have a Durop word that begins with it (only borrowed word) and remains very silent (almost sounding like "b") in the words where it appears.

Papa (n) Papa, a child's name for father

Patirik [from Eng.] (n) Patrick

poris [from Eng.] (n) police

Qq

quai (v) come
e.g. 1. A ka quai? *Will you come?*
2. A quai. [(for a visitor) lit.: "Have you come?"] *Welcome.*

quaini (v) will not come; does not come; am not/is not/are not coming
e.g. 1. N quaini. *I will not come.*
2. O quaini seeng ma. *He/she does not come here.*
3. Be quaini. *They are not coming.*

qun (v) blow continuously (e.g. fire, wind instrument; whistle through the mouth)
e.g. 1. Qun dion dor. *Blow that fire.*
2. A ror u qun iyoyoni? *Do you know how to blow a whistle?*
3. N dorni u qun ndiro. *I don't know how to blow a mouth organ.*

quna (v) tie
e.g. Tum quna durik dor. *Tie that rope well.*

quna kokot (v) [lit.: "tie face"] frown

quni (v) untie

qunn (v) burn or be hot (like pepper)

qunni (adj) burning or hot (like pepper)

quorbere (v) to soften; to make less taut; to calm down

quorna (adj) small, little

quorna uchoormi (n) breathing space.
e.g. Or changhi mmi nke quorna uchoormi. *He/she doesn't give me even a breating space.*

quo [see also kwo] ((adj) this

e.g. Kwen omi quo or ka yeu uromo umorng. *This my child will pass his/her exams.*

quoba (v) slap or beat (slightly and briefly); also to slap a fly or a mosquito

quoi (v) scrape; scrub
1. e.g. Quoi dorkorng dor. *Scrape that pot.*
2. Quoi bunort bungo. *Scrub your nails.*

quooi (v) dry up, dried up (especially a stream, river or pot on the fire)
e.g. 1. Duchai dor du ka fara quooi. *That stream will soon dry up.*
2. A kpanghi korum kor? U kaini ngha dorkorng dor de quooi. *Do you perceive the smell? It seems like that pot has dried up.*

quoop (v) beat, strike
e.g. A sai n ka quop ngo. *If you joke I will beat you.*

qun (v) blow (e.g. a horn or other wind instrument)
e.g. Or dor u qun duyik *He knows how to blow the horn.*

quni (v) blowing
e.g. O quni duyik. *He is blowing the horn.*

quop (v) remove the scales of (e.g. fish)
e.g. Quop ekwem chor. *Remove the scales of that fish.*

quor [see also kwor](adj) that; a word sometimes used to express contempt
e.g.1. Kwen quor or re obaii orne. *That child is a bad person.*
2. U chuwere a quor... *In addition to that...*
3. Quor mmung ndai? *What is this?/ What do you think you are?*

quorn (v) fear; escape from
e.g. 1. Quorn aye, orsa quor. *Fear him/her, that witch/wizard*
2. Or quorn efain ita. *He has escaped from law enforcement officers*

quuna (v) blow (briefly, e.g. fire,or wind instrument); whistle through the mouth)
e.g. Quuna duyik. *Blow the horn.*

quuni (v) wipe; clean
e.g. Quuni nen nengo. *Wipe your eyes.*

Rr

raat (v) [see also daat] sleep
e.g. Or ka raat. *He/she will sleep.*

rama (v) [see also dama] jump (once)
e.g. Or ya u rama. *He likes to jump.*

ramini (v) [see also damini] jumping
e.g. Or ramini mmung? *Why is he/she jumping?*

rara (v) [see also dara] rejoice, jubilate, celebrate
e.g. Or rara mmung? *Why is he/she rejoicing?*

re (inf. v) [see also de] be; am; is; are
e.g. 1. A re mandior? *Are you there?*
2. A re. [lit.: *Are you there?*] *Good afternnoon/Good evening.*

reeni (v) is not, is no; are not, are no; is not available; not present, absent; is nothing; is no bad news
e.g. 1. Kwen ormorng or reeni a enor. *His/her child is not in the house.*
2. Bene be reeni ma. *There are no people here.*
3. Or reeni ndaikwai. *He/she is not present today.*
4. Biain bu reeni a enor. *There is nothing in the house.*
5. Kpara babi esin, biain bu reeni. *Don't panic, there is no bad news.*

reke (v) [see also deke] dirty, make dirty or filthy
e.g. Kpara deke eta aimi. *Don't dirty my clothes.*
(adj) dirty; filthy
e.g. Eyain chai e deke. *This place is dirty.*

rere (adv) [see also dede] still
e.g. Or rere inum. *He/she is still behind.*

rere ning ndior (adv) appprearing so
e.g. Iworn ingo i rere ning ndior i deke deke? *Why are your legs appearing so dirty?*

ri (inf.v) [see also di] will not
e.g. Be ri quai. *They will not come.*

rik (v) [see also dik] return; tinkle (constinuously); tease (a euphemism for)
e.g. 1. A ka fara rik? *Will return soon?*

2. A rik. [(for a resident) [lit.: *Have you returned?*] *Welcome.*

3. Kpara rik kwen quor. *Don't tingle that child.*

riika (v) [see also diika] peep

rika (v) [see also dika] tinkle momentarily; tease (a euphemism for)

riikere (v) [see also diikere] peep; peep into

e.g. A riikere mmung a ubet umi? *Why are you peeipng into my room?*

rima (v) [see also dima] misplace (something); put out (usually a fire or lamp)

roka (v) [see also doka] do a piece of work in instalments

roka kpe (v) pay a debt or a fee in installments

e.g. Or ka roka kpe maruum mengo. *He will pay an installment of your debt.*

roki (v) [see also doki] scrape off or remove quickly from a hole; scoop out from a shell

rokoro (v) fidget; squirm; be restless; be uneasy

ronene nen (v) [see also donene nen] intimidate

rooki (v) [see also dooki] scrape off or remove from a shell

e.g. Nik or nyangha mmi u rooki buchor. *Let him/her help me remove snails from the shells.*

ror (v) [see also dor] know; understand, comprehend

e.g. Or ror din dingo. *He/she knows your name.*

ruki (adj) [see also duki] dangerous

e.g. O ruki. *He/she is dangerous.*

runghene (v) [see also dunghene] investigate; inspect, examine; verify

runghi (v) [see also dunghi] live, living

e.g. 1. O runghi ma. *He/she lives here/He/she is living here.*

ruum (v) [see also duum] rumble (e.g. thunder or stomach), play

ruuma (v) [see also duuma] smell (something), rumbling, playing

Ss

saa (v) sit; sit for
e.g. 1. Saa a bukei. *Sit down.*
2. Saa uromo quor. *Sit for the examinations.*
saaii (adj) silent; quiet; creepy, eerie
e.g. Eyain chai e rere ning ndai saaii? *Why is this place so eerie?*
saaii saaii (adv) silently; quietly
e.g. Saa ma saaii saaii. *Sit here silently.*
sabara (v) reveal, divulge, expose top-secret hidden by means of a physical cover, such as a masquerade
sak (v) tear (e.g. clothes, a book or a paper)
e.g. Kpara a sak nkwet chor. *Don't tear that book.*
sakara (v) rinse; scatter into pieces (for soft fish or some other food item to)
e.g. 1. Sakara nasan nor. *Rinse those plates.*
2. Ekwem chor e sakara a erop. *That fish has scattered into pieces in the soup.*

sai (v) do, did; cause, caused; make, made; joke, joked, play, played; tell e.g. a story
e.g. 1. Sai duwom dungo esin chaini. *Do your work whole-heartedly.*
2. Mmung u sai a ngo a chok? *What made you shout?*
3. Erequa a sai n ka kwop ngo. *If you joke I will beat you.*
4. N keme u sai uke. *I can tell a story.*
sai aikin (v) joke, joking; jest, jesting; tease, teasing
e.g. Or sai aikin. *He/she is joking.*
sai duwom (v) work
e.g. Mmang a sai duwom? *Where do you work?*
saikere kokot (v) frown
e.g. A saikere na meng kokot? *With whom are you frowning?*
saiki (adj) bitter
e.g. Erop chai e saiki. *This soup is bitter.*
sai sai (adv) clearly
e.g. N ya aye, antak or na tangha ukwen sai sai. *I like him/her, because he/she speaks clearly.*
saam (v) send out watery stool

saang (v) disappear, disappeared, vanish, vanished
e.g. Onerom quor or saang. *That man has disappeared.*
saangha (v) disappeared
e.g. Or saangha yen mmang? *Where has he/she disappeared to?*
saanghana (adv) clearly; obviously; evidently; visibly; undoubtedly
e.g. N ning mbe saanghana. *I saw them clearly.*
sana sana [from Efi.] (adj) holy, hallowed
sanghana (v) disappear; dissolve; melt away; evaporate
e.g. 1. Kamaat kaingo ke sanghana kpat. *Your scar has disappeared completely.*
2. Ekwem e sanghana a erop. *The fish has dissolved in the soup.*
sara (adj) thin
e.g. Iworn imorng i sara. *His/her legs are thin.*
sarara (v) gather the remainder of, forage; pick up especially a cutlass by rubbing it against the ground as a strategy to frighen

sarara iworn (v) drag, play delaying tactics
sat (v) scatter; dissolve, especially a meeting
e.g. 1. Kpara sat ndek chor. *Don't scatter the dirt.*
2. Be sat korsorwa kembe. *They have dissolved their meeting.*
sat daban (v) divorce
e.g. Ta be sat daban? *Have they already divorced?*
Satire [from Eng.] (n) Saturday
seei (v) clear, slash
seek (v) laugh
seeki (v) [for many people] laugh; laugh at
seekiri (v) laughing
e.g. A seekiri mmung? *Why are you laughing?*
seeng (v) walk; go
e.g. 1. Fara seeng. *Walk fast.*
2. Seeng kaik. *Go away.*
(adj) sometimes
e.g. A mene seeng munok? *Do you sometimes drink?*
(adv) ever; never; always
e.g. 1. Be quai seeng ma? *Do they ever come here?*
2. Be quaini seeng ma. *They never come here.*
3. N na quai seeng ma a Torsde. *I always come here on Thursday.*

seenghene (v) walk (someone)
e.g. Seenghene kwen quor. *Walk that child.*

seep (v) poison (usually a person)

sen (art.) the
e.g. Bene ba sen a? *Where are the people?*

sengheene (v) maltreat, mistreat, abuse
e.g. Kpara sengheene mbe. *Don't maltreat them.*

sep (v) cut into several pieces, slice
e.g. Nyangha mmi u sep chaap chai. *Help me slice this meat.*

serere (v) level (especially a piece of land or ground)

setan (n) satan

Setemba [from Eng.] (n) September

siba (v) fetch (e.g. water, cooking oil, or garri)

sibiri (v) return (back), make a U-turn or turn round and go back in the direction one is coming from; to turn to a particular part of the body or position; to transform into something
e.g. 1. Fara sibiri dik. *Return home fast.*
2. Sibiri inum. *Turn your back.*
3. Sibiri keyeri. *Turn face-up.*
4. Or keme u sibiri enyi. *He/she can transform into an elephant.*

siika [from Eng.](n) a cigarette; cigarettes

siim (v) send away; dismiss

siim bien (v) expel; deport, repatriate, send home

siira (v) sneeze, sneezed

sika (v) eat (a euphemism for)
e.g. A ka sika biain? *Will you eat something?*

sikere (v) shift

sikere kaik (v) shift away

sikere quai (v) shift nearer

sik sik (adv) early (usually in the moring)
e.g. Quai kito sik sik. *Come early in the morning.*

sim (v) hum

sima (v) push (as in giving birth or excreting); scare away (something or somebody briefly)
e.g. Sima unorn quor. *Scare away that fowl.*

sime (adj) stupid
e.g. Kating a sime? *Are you stupid?*

simini (v) assemble; mix

e.g. Nik i simini ma na koori. *Let's assemble here in the evening.*

2. Simini ita imi na ingo. *Mix your clothes with mine.*

sin (v) refuse; deny

e.g. 1. Kpara a sin kachang kemorng. *Don't refuse his/her gift.*

2. A keme u sin a ubor ungo u reeni a u tibe qu ma? *Can you deny that your hand is in what has just happened here?*

sina (v) seal a hole in a broken area or part; profer greetings, especially in a traditional fashion, to a gathering

sinene (v) seal off, sealed off

e.g. 1. Doboki dor de sinene. *That hole has sealed off.*

2. Doboki da koroi kor de tornghor u sinene. *The hole of that wound has started to seal off.*

riri (v) took care off; fostered; baby-sat

sisi (adj) empty

e.g. Dorkorng daingo de rere sisi? *Is your pot still empty?*

(n) zero

sit (v) take care of (especially a child); to foster; baby-sit

soi (n) a bee; bees; (figurataively) a drunkard ; a dipsomaniac

sokoro (v) cook, prepare (usually soup)

e.g. Or dor u sokooro erop. *He/she knows how to cook soup.*

sookoro (n) an orange; an orange tree

somene (v) wipe (what has been written or drawn); mix

e.g. 1. Adutaina o beke a ami n somene buyairi bu. *The teacher said I should wipe this writing.*

2. Kpara a somene daria daimi na demorng. *Don't mix my food with his/hers.*

sooja [from Eng.](n) a soldier

soorb (v) push (continuously)

e.g. Kpara a soorb kwen quor. *Don't push that child.*

soorbeeree (v) deliberately mispronounce a word or name

e.g. Or ya u soorbeeree din dimi. *He/she is fond of mispronouncing my name.*

Soornghor (n) a very tall person (after the name of a very tall man who once lived in Kororp)

sorb (v) weed

sorba (v) push (briefly); boil (food)

e.g. 1. Kpara sorba bien kwen quor. *Don't push down that child.*

2. Fara sorba chaap chor. *Boil that meat fast.*

sorbere (v) deliberately make a mistake of something; misrepresent someone or give an untrue report of

sork (v) poke (constantly); instigate

e.g. 1. Mmung u se a ngo a sork dubuut dor? *What made you poke at that wall?*

2. Orne o reni or keme u sork mmi u nu na ntem omi. *There is no one who can instigate me to fight with my friend.*

sorka (v) pierce; poke (once or briefly)

e.g. 1. Erequa a seeng dunyor na uta ntume ntume a durum dor, aka sorka ntem ongo a den. *If you go ahead with such a rough play, you will pierce your friend in the eye.*

2. Sorka ket bor chaap chor ta e kwa. *Poke to see if that animal is already dead.*

sorere (v) make lukewarm

sori (v) become warm (e.g. of water, or body to have slight fever)

e.g. 1. Mini mu sori. *The water has become warm.*

2. Baikait ba kwen quo be sori. *This child's body is has become warm.*

sorkere (v) shiver, tremble; be in an unusual haste to do something especially to please

sormene (v) mix, put together

sorne (v) disgrace, humiliate; debase

e.g. Kpara a sorne ibon. *Don't disgrace us.*

soormene (v) erase; deface

e.g. Soormene buyairi bor. *Erase that writing.*

sornghor (v) support; corroborate, second; be older than

e.g. 1. Kwa a sai quor u sornghor ukwen umi. *What you have just done supports my statement.*
2. Okum or beke ibon i tire u dia aye munsop. *Okum said we should stop taking fines from him/her.*
3. Akparika or beke a ibon i tornghot u sop munaii. Nkum or sornghor. *Akparika said we should start ciontributing money. Nkum seconded.*
4. Ominkei ongo or sornghor mmi. *Your brother/sister is older than me.*

soror (adj) for something to be warm
e.g.1. Baikait ba kwen quo be soror. *This child's body is warm.*
2. Mini mu mun soror. *This water is warm.*

suk (v) rear (especially domestic animals)
e.g. M biri yau u suk nornorn. *I would like to rear chicken.*

suka (v) hook, pull the hook line to catch a fish

sukere (v) relax; calm down, pipe down; humble (oneself or someone)

e.g. 1. Sukere baikait baingo. *Calm yourself down.*
2. Erequa a sukere baikait, Obasi or ka bairere ngo. *If you humble yourself, God will exalt you.*

suorp (n) soap

suu (v) lie, say something that is untrue
e.g. Kpara suu nne. *Don't lie to me.*

suuk (v) hook; catch fish by pulling the hookline

suuka (n) sugar

suwa (v) pin (especially a stick), pitch (e.g. a tent or hut)

Tt

ta (v) take the lead or first position; has/have already
e.g. 1. Ta dunyor. *Take the lead*
2. Mmi n ta dunyor uromo. *I took first in the exams.*
3. N ning ma ta chun. *I can see that you have finished.*

ta (v) have...yet; have...already
e.g. 1. Ta a dia biain? *Have you eaten something yet?*
2. Ta be beke *Have they already arrived.*

taaina (v) teach; train; display; demonstrate
e.g. Taaina mbe kwa a kpewiri. *Teach them what you have learnt.*

taak (v) remain, has remained; confined; stuck
e.g. A kwaka a mi n taak ma? *Do you want me to remain here?*

taang (v) to talk, to speak
e.g. Taang nnangha. *Speak then.*

taangha (v) step over

taani (v) smeer
e.g. Kpara a taani munei mor a dubut. *Don't smear that oil on the wall.*

taaik (v) swear (repeatedly); swearing

taa ree (v) was, was once; were, were once
e.g. 1. N taa ree andiom orne. *I was a slim person.*
2. I taa ree ikpor uyin. *We were once a big family.*

taba (v) follow, go behind (someone), go after (someone); understand

taika (v) swear (once or briefly)

taaim (v) to dish (food into plates), dishing
e.g. Ama omi ortornghor u taim daria. *My mother has started dishing the food.*

taaimene (v) measure something to know the quantity
e.g. Taaimene kari kor ko ibon i dor ibat a korp. *Measure the garri so we know the number of cups.*

taimaine (v) to take someone's measurements

taina (v) show, showed; signify, signified; portray, protrayed
e.g. 1. Taina mbe eyain asen. *Show them the place.*

2. Ukwen quor u taina mmung? *What does that statement signify?*
3. Kwa a beke ndior u taina a ngo a de ochu. *What you just said portrays you as a thief.*
taina ainain (v) guide
taina baikait (v) show off
e.g. Or ya u taina baikait. *He/she likes to show off.*
tak (v) chew; masticate
taki (v) chewing; masticating
tana (inf.v) plan
e.g. A tata tana u quai na ibon? *Did you earlier plan to come with us?*
ta neye (adv) until now, up until now, to date
e.g. N na ning aye ta neye. *I have not seen him/her up until now.*
tangha (v) swear, to ask for juju's intervention against someone
tap (v) reach
Taa a tap enor? *Have you reached the house yet?*
tara (v) stagger
tari (v) slide, slip
tawa (v) put down
e.g. Tawa ekpaime chor okpokoro. *Put that bottle on the table.*
tawet [from Eng.] (n) towel

te (v) smash (e.g. potato)
teekeere (v) welcome (especially by hailing) happily
teeng (v) stagger
e.g. Nik ononoki quor or teeng yen. *Let that drunkard stagger away.*
tem (v) curse someone; choke
e.g. 1. Kpara a tem aye. *Don't curse him/her.*
2. Dia duchorn ko a be tem. *Eat slowly so you don't choke.*
tenghe (v) step aside
e.g. O nining mmi ndai, or tenghe chang mmi ainain. *As soon as he/she saw me, he/she stepped aside to give me the way.*
teu (v) step on (someone); smash with the feet (e.g. muddy ground for building the walls of a house); give many incisions to
e.g. 1. Kpara a teu nne iworn. *Don't step on my feet.*
2. Baton be ror u teu bukei ba bubeet kpai borom. *Women know how to smash the earth for mudding walls with the feet more than men.*

3. Nik or teu kikuk kor ko ke sanghana. *Let him/her incise the lump so that it disappears.*

tewe (v) step on; incise (once or briefly)

tii (n) [from Eng.] tea

tiikere (v) deceive; frighten (continuously)
e.g. A tiikere meng? *Who are you deceiving?*

tiina (n) write; draw (espeacially a line)

tian (n) zinc, corrugated iron sheets; a basin

tibe (inf. v) happen, occur, transpire, arise

tibiri (v) reward for an entertainment received
e.g. U normi u tibiri bornornormi. *It is nice to reward dancers.*

tik (v) urge on, persuade, force to act
e.g. 1. Kpara a tik nne u ba aye. *Don't persuade me to marry him/her.*
2. Kpara a tik aye u men munok. *Don't force him to drink.*

tikere (v) frighten; deceive (momentarily)

tikiri (v) tremble, shiver
e.g. Ini a burieu bu ka kuba aye or ka tikiri. *When fear will grip him/he he/she will tremble.*

tinghene (v) stiffen, cause to become stiff or erect; flex (especially muscles)

tinghi (v) become stiff; become erect

tini (v) rub against

tire (v) end; stop
e.g. Tire u koon din dimi. *Stop calling my name.*

tiri (v) for food not to cook well; for a woman to become infertile
e.g. 1. Erequa a biri tum kporkere dion dor, borkor bor be ka tiri. *If you don't make the fire well, the food will not cook well.*
2. Orkporsong a kamarin o sai ben baton baibon be tiri. *It is excessive use of gamalin that has made our young women become infertile.*

toi buuna (v) prune, trim (that is, cut the branches of a plant)
e.g. Erequa a kwka koorfi kaingo ke tum chim, toi buuna ini ini. *If you want your coffee to bear well, prune the braches from time to time.*

toki (v) pinch (momentarily); get up from a squatting position

toi (v) remove one after another; ostracise, excommunicate; lift a (e.g. a ban), repeal; peck (continuously)
e.g. 1. Toi ichap nyor ekpa. *Remove the meat from the bag.*
2. Be toi Ojom Ekwe. *They have ostracized Ojom from Ekwe.*
3. Be chorm u toi kibain kor. *They need to lift/repeal that ban/injunction.*
4. Orman unorn kwor u ka toi aye. *That hen will peck him/her.*

tonghene (v) nod off, nodding off (especially as a result of feeling sleepy)
e.g. Or tornghor u tonghene. *He/she has started nodding off.*

toni (v) repair, fix (done quickly)
(adv) carefully
e.g. Toni mort ekpaime chor. *Handle that bottle carefully.*

tooka (v) squat; land, perch (e.g. a bird)
e.g. Borng kpat itort nyor i tooka. *Wait until that bird perches.*

tooki (v) pinch (continuously)

tooni (v) repair, fix carefully; make, manufacture

toonini (v) repairing, repaired; fixing, fixed; making, made; manufacturing, manufactured
e.g. A toonini mmung ma? *What are you repairing here?*

toora (v) get glued to (e.g. a snail)
e.g. Ket arangha echor e toora a kana ka kainaii kor. *A snail has gotten glued to the branch of that tree.*

toorere (v) narrate, relate; explain
e.g. Toorere arangha u tibe. *Narrate how it happened.*

toori (v) pick (e.g. a louse); fetch (especially fire)
e.g. Or ya u toori dion a kiichin omi. *He/she likes to fetch fire from my kitchen.*
(adj) hot
e.g. 1. Dion du du toori kpai. *This fire is too hot.*
2. N ya mini mu toori. *I like hot water.*

toorka (v) hang (oneself)

e.g. A kwaka u toorka kwa? *Do you want to hang yourself dead?*

toornghi (v) drip (continuously)

toornghini (v) dripping

e.g. Mini mu toornghini ma. *Water is dripping here.*

toort (adj) hot

e.g. Dion bu toort. *The fire is so hot.*

(v) get hot

e.g. Nik mini mor mun tum toork. *Let that water get hot well.*

tor (v) remove (at once); take (e.g. a photo); subtract; commit (e.g. an abortion or terminate a pregnancy); name (e.g. a child)

e.g. 1. Tor unaan quor a ainain. *Remove that stone from the road.*

2. Tor mmi foto. *Take a photograph of me.*

3. Or tor buqun. *She has committed an abortion.*

4. Be kwaka u tor kwen quor din. *They want to name that child.*

tora (v) put something into fire

e.g.1. Tora idiaii nyor kpat i don. *Put that cutlass into the fire until it gets red hot.*

torbere (v) cause to become muddy or turbid (e.g. by adding too much water); overcook, cooking to become too soft

e.g. Kpara a torbere desi dor. *Don't overcook that rice.*

torbi (v) become muddy, turbid, too soft, or watery

torere (v) heat (especially food)

e.g. Seeng de torere daria daimi. *Go and heat my food.*

tori (v) pinch (e.g. meat)

e.g. Kwen quo or ya u tori chaap ore ochu. *A child who likes to pinch meat is a thief.*

toritort (adj) hot

e.g. N ya tii or toritort. *I like hot tea.*

torka (v) tether, chain; hang (someone or something)

e.g. 1. Tum torka ebon chor. *Tether that goat well.*

2. Be kwaka u torka aye? *Do they want to hang him/her?*

tornghor (v) start, begin, commence

e.g. Meng or ka tornghor? *Who will start?*

163

(adv) since

e.g. Tornghor ini nyor or na quai daing ma. *Since that time he/she has not come here again.*

tornghor tornghor (adv) since, ever since

e.g. Tornghor tornghor orba tung ma, n na ning aye daing. *Ever since he/she left here I have not seen him/her again.*

Torsdai [from Eng.] (n) Thursday

tortoort (adj) hot

e.g. Dia be tortoort. *Eat it hot.*

tor usene (v) retaliate, revenge

e.g. N ka tor usene. *I will retaliate.*

tornghi (v) drip (once or a few times)

tornghene (v) drop (for instance a small quantity of oil, water or drink into a container); drop a liquid into the eye (such as eye drop)

tou (v) plant, cultivate, sow

e.g. N ka tornghor u tou ekpang aingo kwanaka. *I will start planting your farm soon.*

toui (v) planting; sowing; cultivating

e.g. O toui mmung? *What is he/she planting/sowing/cultivatig?*

towa (v) plant, sow (to do so momentarily)

toya (v) peck at

e.g. Arequa a ruma na orman unorn quor u ka toya ngo. *If you play with that hen it will peck at you.*

tikere (v) deceive; mislead

e.g. A kwaka u tikere mmi? *Do you want to deceive me?*

tui (v) wake two or more people from sleep; rinse a container with a small opening by putting water into it and shaking; spit (repeatedly)

e.g. 1. Ben bor be rere a kornorngha kpat arangakwo? Tui mbe! *Those whildren are still in bed up till now? Wake them up!*

2. Tui desip dor a ba korn orkem quor etaing. *Ring the calabash before you put the palm wine into it*

3. Or ya u tui bunyorni. *He is fond of spitting out saliva*

tuk (v) divide, share; grate (especially cassava for gari or cocoyam for ekpang)

e.g. 1. Tuk biain ikie iyain inai. *Divide one hundred things by four.*
2. Tuk chang kporkporor orne. *Share it to everybobdy.*

tuka (v) for people to divide or share something among themselves
e.g. Tuka nor daria dor mboon na mboon. *Share that food amongst yourselves.*

tukere (v) for a few people to share something between or among themselves; to maltreat someone
e.g. 1. Mbork, tukere nor kworna daria dor. *Please, share that little food.*
2. Kpara tukere onaton quor. *Don't maltreat that woman.*

tum (v) pound (especially fufu); beat or pound; make (especially a bed)
e.g. 1. N ka tum ngo ngha arangha be tumi bumang. *I will pound you the way fufu is pounded.*
3. Kpara tum kwen quor. *Don't beat that child.*
4. Or ror u tum bunang. *He/she knows how to pound fufu*
5. Tum kornorngha kaimi. *Make my bed.*
(conj) unless, except
e.g. 1 Be beke a mbe be baariri, tum mboon bu numa mbe eti a dormorn. *They said they won't leave, unless you send them a good word.*
(adv) well, carefully; properly; thoroughly; meticulously
e.g. 1. Tum mort kwen quor. *Hold that child carefully.*
2. Tum choork. *Grind thoroughly.*

tuma (v) pound (briefly)

tume (v) attempt; try; endeavour; struggle
e.g. Tume nyenene. *Try again.*

tumene (v) confuse, make someone to forget
e.g. Kpara tumene mmi. *Don't confuse me.*

tuna (v) give back, return something taken, borrowed or stolen; repay, refund, reimburse money borrowed or stolen
e.g. N ka tuna daria daingo. *I will return your food.*

tunene (v) push (e.g. a truck or vehicle)

tung (v) go out (especially from an enclosure such as a house or a car); leave a particular place or group

tung daban (v) divorce (usually for one party to leave the marriage home)
e.g. U noormi u tung daban. *It is not good to divorce.*

tunghene (v) bring something or somebody out of hiding; bring out a masquerade on public display

tung quai (v) appear; materialize

turere (v) arch out the buttocks by bending slightly

turi (adj) blunt
e.g. Idiaii nyi i turi kpai. *This cutlass is too blunt.*

tura (v) arch out the buttocks by bending slightly
(adj) the body not generally smart due to drowsiness from previous night's sleeplessness, feeling of premonition, or impending illness
e.g. Kpara nyi duwom erequa a baikait be tura ngo. *Don't go to work if your body is not smart enough.*

tut (v) pour out (e.g. a liquid from a big container with a small opening)
e.g. Tut munok mor ma a mbam. *Pour out the wine in the jug.*

tut bien (v) pour away
e.g. Tut bien mini mor. *Pour away that water.*

Tusdai [from Eng.] (n) Tuesday

tuubi (v) become extremely foolish

tuuk (v) cheat
e.g. Or ya u tuuk bene. *He/she likes to cheat people.*

tuuma (v) encounter; cross one's path

tuunghi (v) germinate, germinated; for a dead and buried person to be appearing
e.g. 1. Mbangsang etornhor u tunghi. *The groundnuts are already germinated.*
2. Ornerom quor or qua or ka tuunghi. *If that man dies he will be appearing.*

tuura (v) pour liquid from a big container with a small opening (briefly and fast)
e.g. Tuura quona a munei a desip dor. *Pour a little oil from that calabash.*

tuurere (v) make sharp object blunt;
e.g. Kpara a turere idiaii imi. *Don't make my cutlass blunt.*

tuuya (v) wake someone up from sleep; rinse (e.g. a bottle containing water by shaking)
e.g. 1. Kpara a tuuya mmi, kpat u tap nkarika inan. *Don't wake me until it strikes 3 O'clock.*
2. Tuuya ekpaime chor a ba kain munei mor. *Rinse that bottle before pour in in that oil.*

tuya (v) spit, spat

Uu

u (prep) to
e.g. 1. A kwaka u sai mmung? *What do you want to do?*
2. Ukwen kwu u bura nning? *What does this statement mean?*
(v) how to; is; has, had
e.g. 1. N dorni u chiork. *I don't know how to swim.*
(pro) it (but the "it" is redundant in some translated sentences)
1. Mmung u re mandio? *What is there?*
2. Kwen unorn u re a kornorn ka bekork bengo. *There is a chicken under your bed.*
3. Ukwen u deni. *There is no problem.*
4. Orom unorn quor u ri quai daing. *That cock will not come again.*
5. U re nning? *How is it?*

ubakara inum (n) betrayal
e.g. Atata anduki ubakara inum nde. *This is the most dangerous betrayal ever.*

ubangha (adj) about, concerning
e.g. A kpang ukwen ubangha mmi? *Have you heard any discussion concerning me?*

ubaii (n) sin, evil, badness
e.g. Ubaii u chawi kpai nkang a kaibain. *There is too much sin on earth.*

ubaima (n) acceptance
uben (n) boundary
ubet (n) room
ubia ibat (n) pride
ubinghene baikait (n) condenscention; humility
ubini (n) ebony
ubo (n) kolanut tree
ubok (n) a hole (in the ground)
uboong (n) floor mat
uboonghene (n) aimless wandering
ubor (n) hand, arm
ubor inum (n) bribe or bribes; bribery, corruption
e.g. 1. U noormi u dia ubor inum. *It is not good to take bribes.*
2. Ubor inum u noormi. *Bribery is not good.*

uboror a baikait (n) [lit.: body response] sense (e.g. of smell, touch, etc)

ubowa ini (n) delay, hesitation; procrastination

ubura (inf. v) it means

uchaina (n) greetings; salutation; compliments

uchamana (n) an embrace; the act of embracing or cuddling

uchari (n) bitter kola tree

uchoormi (n) breath; the act of breathing; breathing sound
e.g. 1. E kwa bor e chorchorm kworna uchoormi? *Is it dead or does it still have some breath?*

uchuna daban (n) divorce

uchuwere (adv) additionally, additional to, in addition to
e.g. 1. Uchuwere mandior. *Additional to that/ additionally*
2. Uchuweere a quor. *In addition to that.*

uda ikang [from Efi.] (n) a match; a match box

udeme [from Efi.] (n) a share; a share one has in a business; a portion; concern
e.g. 1. Chang udeme umi. *Give my share.*
2. Or chorm udeme a kombani quor. *He/she has a share in that company.*
3. A chorm udeme ekpang chor? *Do you have a portion in that farm.*
4. Udeme ungo a ukwen quor a? *What is your concern in that matter?*

udiana (adj) second, next, additional, in addition to
e.g. Udiana a ukwen u de… *The second point is…*

udoribot (n) a pillow

udunghene (n) investigation, inspection, examination for medical purposes or for verification of the truth about something or somebody

ududu [from Efi.] (n) power, authority; courage, boldness; audacity; effrontery
e.g. 1. Ududu Orbasi u kpai ududu a setan. *The power of God is more than the power of satan*
2. Or chormi ududu u sim mbe ma. *He/she has no authority to send them away from here.*
3. Meng or chang ngo ududu a ngo a sa a korsorwa kaimi ka duborn? *Who gave you the*

audacity to sit on my throne?
ufaikaiyo [from Efi.] (n) an umbrella
ufang [fromEfi.] (n) a space, breathing space; a chance, an opportunity
ufat nkpor [from Efi.] (n) scissors
ufen [from Efi.] (n) suffering, sufferings
ufia [from Efi.] (n) a slap
ufiaip [from Efi.] (n) fever that raises body temperature
ufikiri (n) verification, cross-cheking, cross-validation, confirmation
e.g. N kwaka ufikiri a ukwen quu. *I want verification in this issue.*
uforn [from Efi.] (n) profit, gain, benefit; point
e.g. 1. Uforn ungo a? *What's your benefit?*
2. Uforna a? *What's the point?*
ufort (n) middle, centre (adj) middle or central position
ufup (n) jealousy
e.g. Or ya kpai ufup. *He/she is too fond of jealousy.*

uka (adv) yet, for now; for a while; at the moment
e.g. 1. N di kwai uka. *I won't come yet.*
2. Boorng uka. *Wait for a while.*
3. Nik i koom nyindior uka. *Let's leave it like that at the moment.*
ukan (n) a message
e.g. Meng o numa ngo ukan qu? *Who sent you this message?*
ukani (n) a huge log of wood (especially across a path or road)
Ukapedisua [from Efi.] (n) Christmas
ukaara (n) curtain (especially of Ekwe or a grand, public ocassion
uke (n) a story; a tale
e.g. Meng or ka sai uke? *Who will tell a story?*
ukem (adj) equal, enough
ukem ukem [from Efi.] (adv) equally
e.g. Tuk daria dor ukem ukem. *Share that food equally.*
ukaini ngha (v) it looks like, it seems
uko [from Efi.] (n) show of power or strength
ukom (n) a tree, locally known as "njasanga" or "njangsang", with hard-

shelled seeds used as soup thickener and flavouring

ukork (n) chewing stick

ukot (n) a shadow; silhouette

ukort (n) raffia palm; raffia palm wine

ukpangha (n) a bolt; a lock

ukpangha a itum (n) a door bolt; a door lock

ukparara (n) dilly-dallying, dragging of legs, procrastination
e.g. N yani ukparara a biain bu. *I don't like procrastination on this issue.*

ukpono [from Efi.] (n) respect; honour
e.g. Chang Obasi ukpono. *Give honour to God.*

ukporkere [from Efi.] (n) a key
e.g. Dorkin dai de chormi ukporkere. *This lock has no key.*

ukporng (n) soul, spirit

ukut (n) hardship; disrespect, an expression of condescension, high and mighty
eg. 1. Ukuk u ka choon aye. *Hardship will kill him/her.*
2. N yani ukut. *I don't like disrespect.*
(inj) An expression of surprise or disgust why a particular behaviour should be expressed towards or in the presence of one.
e.g. Ukut a mmung? or Ukut u mi eh! or ket nor ukut! *High and mighty!*

ukwak ukwen (n) the act of looking for trouble; aggressiveness; antagonism

ukwau (n) ampit

ukwen (n) a word, a talk, a speech, a statement; a problem, an issue; a point; a matter; a case
e.g. I ka yau ngo a chaang ibon ukwen. *We will like you to give us a speech.*

ukworkirinua [from Efi.] (n) a handkerchief

umi (pro) my, mine

unaan (n) a pebble, a rock

unan (n) a wound, an injury; under hard struggle
e.g. 1. Or chorma unan? *Has he/she sustained an injury?*
2. Unan or ba baima. *It was under hard struggle before he/she accepted.*

unap (n) scarcity, shortage; lack
e.g. A dia biain ndaikwai, kere ini unap. *As you eat today, think of times of scarcity.*

unap a mini (n) water scarcity
e.g. Unap a mini in re ma na konum. *Water scarcity is rapant here in the dry season.*

unap a ichap (n) wildlife (animal) depopulation, wildlife scarcity
e.g. I tornghor u ning unap a ichap ma. *We are beginning to experience wildlife scarcity here.*

unau (n) a thigh

unem (n) chalk (what is popularly known as Calabar chalk); a traditional form of blessings by rubbing Calabar chalk on one's hand; (also figuratively) blessings
e.g. 1. Baton ba Kororp be ya u korma unem. *Kororp women like rubbing Calabar chalk.*
2. Amene a mene ormorng or korn aye unem [lit.: His/her great grand father has rubbed him/her with Calabar chalk]. *His/her grand father has given him blessings.*
3. Ndaikwai daikwai da unem umi. *Today is the day of my blessings.*

unen (n) right, rights (as in human rights), what is true, correct and acceptable
e.g. M baat a unen umi. *I stand for my rights.*
(adj) straightforward, doing what is right
e.g. Or re orne a unen. *He/she is a straightforward person.*

ungwingha (n) a hint
e.g. Nke ungwingha a be ka quai? *Not even a hint that they will come?*

urori (n) profit, gain
e.g. A chorm urori a okum kwo? *Do you make profit in this business?* [lit.: Do you have profit in this business?]

unoi (n) shea nut or poga tree whose seeds are used to produce edible oil

unorm (n) an unexpected or unprepared for responsibility or burdern

unoorm (n) goodluck, blessings, success, prosperity
e.g. Diet du du re ini a unoorm a enor aimi. *This year is a year of prosperity in my family.*
unorn (n) a chicken
unorn a orkat (n) a duck
unum (n) errand; the act of sending someone on an errand
e.g. 1. N de unum. *I am on an errand.*
2. Or ya kpai nkang unum. *He/she is too fond of sending someone on an errand.*
unwham (n) help, support, facilitation
e.g. Mbork, chaang aye unwham. *Please, give him/her help.*
unwingha (n) a hint; forewarning
e.g. N chorma unwingha a baifain ba enork be ka quai ma. *I got a hint that soldiers will come here.*
unwor (n) a camwood tree
unwornghor (n) an oath
e.g. A keme u dia unwornghor a ukwen quor? *Can you take an oath on that issue?*
unyorm (n) a bush mango tree

ureme [from Efi.] (n) a share; shares, portion, portions, allocation, allocations
u re a ikpain (v) to be alive
e.g. U re a ikpain u re unem a Orbasi. *To be alive is God's blessings.*
uremi (n) a whisper; whispering
e.g. Quai i chorma quorna a uremi. *Come and let's have a little whisper.*
urika (n) a peep; the act of peeping
e.g. Urika quor u bura nning? *What does that peeping mean?*
uromo [from Efi.] (n) a test, an examination, exams; temptation, temptations
e.g. Ikpain i chawi uromo. *Life is full of temptations.*
uroribot [from Efi.] (n) a pillow
urum (n) forest; environment
urum a beem (n) a jungle
urum a kormborm (n) a jungle
urum a nyen (n) a virgin forest
urung (n) morter
usan (n) a pan; a bowl

usani (n) sand (also eupehism for gari)
usani usani (adj) sandy
e.g. Bukei bu bu re usani usani. *This soil is sandy.*
usan a ikot (n) a plate
usaing (n) excretment; faeces; stool; the bathroom (euphemism for going to stool)
e.g. 1. U korni u ning usaing a anwha. *It is his difficult to see the excrement of a cat.*
2. N kwaka u nyi usaing. *I want to go to the bathroom.*
usat daban (n) divorce
e.g. Be ki de a usat daban. *They are now facing divorce.*
useeng a ntak chor (conj) for that reason, consequently, as a result, in view of that, therefore, hence
e.g. O biri kona nne, useeng a ntak chor n di quai. *He/she did't invite me, for that reason I won't come.*
usene (n) retaliation, revenge; pay back; replacement
e.g. 1. M baat a usene. *I stand for revenge.*
2. N ka chang ngo usene a ekpaime a m biani. *I will give you a replacement for the bottle that I broke.*
usiritorng (n) tonsillitis; a trap or traps set to catch animals by the neck
usobo (n) loin-cloth (of normal size)
usoror [from Efi.] (v) a celebration
e.g. I re a usoror ndaikwai. *We are in celebration today.*
uta (n) type, kind, sort
e.g. Utor a biain bu bu noormi. *This sort of thing is not good.*
utaba (n) ground tobacco, "snuff"
utaimene (n) measurement; the act of measuring
e.g. A ba utaimene umorng? *Have you taken his/her measurement?*
utana (n) way; side; over
e.g. 1. N nyi utana nquni? *Which way do I go?*
2. Utana nquni a ya? *Which side do you prefer?*
2. A chorm dion utana quor. *Do you have fire over there.*
utang (n) the lowest part of the barn at the fire place, mainly used for drying meat, fish and other items

utchoormi (n) breathing, breath
utchoorni (n) snoring
utaina baikait (n) showiness, ostentation
utaip (n) hunting
utikere (n) deception, deceit
utonikang [from Efi.] (n) a lamp
e.g. Baaira utonikang quor. *Light that lamp.*
utonikang a eyang (n) carbide lamp
utooni (n) repair, mending; fixing; fabrication, manufacturing
utorere (n) a statement; an explanation
e.g. 1. Chang utorere ungo. *Give your statement.*
2. N kwaki anyiri utorere. *I don't want a long explanation.*
utor (n) type, kind, sort, brand
e.g. Utor nquni a kwaka. *Which type/kind/brand do you want?*
utori (n) pinching; pilfering
e.g. 1. Utori u de uchu. *Pinching is stealing.*
2. Utori u noormi. *Pilfering is not good.*
utuk (n) cheating

e.g. Utuk u noormi. *Cheating is not good.*
utume (n) attempt; trial; endeavour; struggle
utung (n) frontyard (adv) outside
u tunghi a (conj) through; because of; happening in the name of
e.g. U tunghi a kwen ongo, Omuna obon, Yises Kraisi. *Through your son, our Lord, Jesus Christ.*
u tunghi ning (adv) How come it that
e.g. U tunghi ning ko be dion ma qua I biri ning mbe. *How come it that they entered here without us seeing them.*
uurim (n) ill-luck, bad luck, hard luck, misfortune
uukara (n) tenure of office, rule; rulership, leadership
e.g. Ekese a aiti a borkor be tibe ini a uukara umonrg. *Many good things happened during his/her tenure of office.*
uukot (v) inlaw
uuraan (n) a monitor lizard
uwab eba [from Efi.] (n) breast-wear

uwakara (n) a junction; a Y-junction; a T-junction; crossroads: a bifurcation; a confluence; an intersection

uwam (n) hook

uwan (n) a canoe

uwan inchin (n) (lit: engine canoe) engine boat; speed boat

uwana [from Efi.] (n) group, association, connection, partnership e.g. Or chorm uwana na ibon. *He/she has partnership with us.*

uwara (n) a loan, loans

uwom (n) the highest female traditional society in Kororp, known as in Efik as "Ekpa"

uworn (n) leg

uyai [from Efi.] (n) a decoration; a spectacle; splendour

uyang (n) dribbling (especially with a ball); hanky-panky (also used figuratively to mean)

uyeen (n) a plum tree

uyei (n) moon; month; menses

uyin (n) family (including the extended type)

uyire (n) insistence, the habit of egging on

Ww

wai (v) name; disclose (e.g. those involved in an act); split (especially wood); saw (especially wood)

waan (v) lay or stay in wait; ambush; set a trap against someone

waaiki (v) gnaw, eat like a rat (continuously)

waaikiri (v) gnawing

waari (v) pick the teeth (especially with a toothpick)

waiki (v) gnaw, eat like a rat (momentarily)

wain (v) be or stay long; last long
e.g. 1. N di wain. *I won't be long.*
2. Daria dai de di wain. *This food won't last long.*

wakara (v) separate; bifurcate; branch off
e.g. I ka wakara a uwakara uruk. *We shall separate at the next junction.*

waki (v) reduce the quantity of
e.g. Waki daria daimi. *Reduce my food.*

wana (v) associate; connect, partner, have something to do with
e.g. Nik I wana na mbe ko i tum sai duworm du. *Let's partner with them so that we do this job more effectively.*

wang (adj) many
e.g. Ichap iwang? *How many animals?*

wap (adv) quick

wap wap (adv) expeditiously, fast, quickly, rapidly, speedily; hurriedly, hastily
e.g. N na sai duwom dumi wap wap. *I do my work expeditiously.*

wara (v) stick (especially between a gap or crevice); borrow; lend
e.g. 1. Wara dukoko dor a itam ingo. *Stick that feather on your hat.*
2. Or wara mmi ekese a munaii. *He/she borrowed a lot of money from me.*
3. N wara aye ekese a munaii. *I loaned him a lot of money.*

wari (v) take something from a gap or crevice

waya [from Eng.] (n) wire; a snare, a trap

week (v) to burn out (especially fuelwood or candle)

e.g. Imet imi i week kpat. *My fuelwood has burnt out completely.*

wekere (v) cause to burn out (especially fuelwood, by using much at a time)

e.g. Kpara a wekere imet imi. *Don't burn out my fuelwood.*

Wenesdai [from Eng.] (n) Wednesday

werere (v) shift

werere kaik (v) shift, shift away

werere quai (v) shift nearer

wha (v) butcher

e.g. N dorni u wha chaap. *I don't know how to butcher an animal.*

wiba (v) fasten, tighten (adj) tight

e.g. Munkpakot mu mu wiba kpai. *These shoes are too tight.*

wiima (v) sprinkle, spray; swear to juju by spraying, for instance, "alligator pepper"

wiira (v) sipping, sucking; syphoning

e.g. Ket arangha kwen ongo o wiira mumbai ma ama. *See how your child is sucking the mothers breasts.*

wira (v) sip; syphon

wiriri (v) pour

e.g. 1. Wiriri busani bor ma. *Pour that sand here.*
2. Mini mun ka wiriri. *The rain will pour.*

wiriri bien (v) pour out

wiriri mini (v) baptize; be baptized

e.g. 1. Faara or ka wiriri ngo mini. *The Reverend Father will baptise you.*
2. N wiriri mini. *I am baptised.*

wok (v) confess; give a testimony about a bad act, such as involving in witchcraft and committing an adultery

e.g. Ornaton quor or wok ubaii umorng. *That woman has confessed her sins.*

woka (v) fall, fallen (especially unripe fruits); shed (especially for a tree to drop its leaves)

e.g. 1. Echimi a kanaii kai ai wiriri. *The fruits of this tree have fallen.*
2. Kainaii kai ke wiriri ikwang imorng. *This tree has shed its leaves.*

won (v) father a child

woni (v) has fathered a child

e.g. Mmeng o woni ngo. *Who has fathered you?*

woong (v) cry
Kpara woong. *Don't cry.*

woongha (v) crying
e.g. A woongha mmung? *Why are you crying?*

wook (v) scratch (gently, especially an itching paart of the body)

wooka (v) scratching (gently)
e.g. A wooka mmung baikait nyindior. *Why are you scratching your body like that?*

woora (v) near; approach
e.g. Saa woora na me. *Sit near me.*
(adj) near
e.g. O biri dung woora ma. *He/she does not leave near here.*

woororor (v) drop, drops (on its own because it is over-size, e.g. trousers or skirk)
e.g. Anyiri iwoorn omi or woororor. *My trousers drops.*

wori (v) leave, get out of
e.g. Wori ma aranghaquo! *Leave here now!/Get out of here now!*
(adj) not near
e.g. Ornaton kwor o wori ma. *That woman is not near here.*

work (v) dandle
e.g. Work kwen quor ko o tire u woong. *Dandle that child so that it stops to cry.*

wororor (v) pull down
e.g. 1. Wororor anyiri iwoorn ongo. *Pull down your trousers.*

woorki (v) grow weak to fainting point; droop (e.g. leaves)

woorn (v) decay; rot; decompose; putrefy
e.g. Erequa a biri tum changhana chaap chor e ka woorn. *If you don't dry that meat well it will decay.*

wot (adj) near
e.g. A wot ma? *Are you near here?*

wuou (v) burn; roast; distill (hot drink)
e.g. 1. Be tornghor u wuou bukpang bumbe. *They have started to burn their farm plots.*

2. Tum wuou chaap chor. *Roast that meat well.*

3. Or ror u wuou munok. *He/she knows how to distil hot drink.*

Yy

ya (v) like; prefer; love; be fond of
e.g. 1. Or ya u rung ma. *He/she likes to live here.*
2. A ya nkwoni? *Which do you prefer?*
3. Or ya mmi. *He/she loves me.*
4. Or ya u seeng a dubam da orkpa. *He/she is fond of walking on the river bank.*

yaaii (v) decorate
e.g. Seeng be yaaii ngo. *Go and let them decorate you.*

yaaim (v) stay awake all night; keep vigil

yaaka (v) stick, get stuck on something, stand pressed against something (such as a wall)
e.g. 1. Ekpai e yaaka a mini ma orkpor. *A rat is stuck in latex.*
2. Be baat yaaka a dubut kpat i seeng yeu kwa i biri ning mbe. *They stood pressed against the wall until we walked past without seeing them.*

yaang (n) tree pangolin

yaani (v) don't like
e.g. N yaani aye. *I don't like him/her.*

yai (v) become flat (especially a drink)
e.g. Orkem quo or yai. *This palm wine is flat.*

yaiba (v) wander, wander about, wandering, wandering about

yain (v) hate
e.g. Kpara a yain mmi. *Don't hate me.*

yaing (v) cut; cut short, interrupt
e.g. 1. Yaing kainaii kai. *Cut this stick.*
2. Kpara a yaing ukwen umi. *Don't interrupt my speech.*

yaing nkaim (v) circumcise
e.g. A ikwai changhachanhanai be ka yaing kwen quor nkaim. *In eight days' time they will circumcise that child.*

yaini (v) don't hate; wake up (from sleep)
e.g. 1. N yaini aye. *I don't hate him/her.*
2. A ka fara yaini diyain? *Will you wake up early tomorrow?*
3. A yaini. [lit.: Have you woken up?] *Good morning.*

yaira (v) take down, write, written (quickly)
e.g. Orbasi, mbork, yaira din dimi a nkwet a ikpain. *God, please, write my name in the book of life.*

yait (v) write; draw
e.g. A keme u yait buyairi? [lit: Can you write writing?] *Can you write?*

yang (v) dribble; (also used figuratively) deceive
e.g. 1. A keme u yang mmi na borl? *Can you dribble me with the ball?*
2. A kemeni u yang orne ngha mmi. *You cannot dribble/deceive a person like me.*

yarara (v) reveal, divulge, expose a top-secret
e.g. Mbork kpara a yarara aidiaimi aibon. *Please, don't reveal our plan.*

yau (v) love; feel affection for
e.g. Yau aton ngo ngharangha a ya baikait baingo. *Love your wife as much as you love yourself.*

yebere (v) dodge; avoid meeting someone or something
e.g. A biri koom neen na ochu quo or ka yebere u ngwei. *If you don't keep watch over that thief, he/she dodge to escape.*

yeei (v) shout at or bark at repeatedly
e.g. Kpara a yeei ben bor. *Don't shout at those children.*

yeeke (v) carry on the shoulder
e.g. Ket arangha n ka yeeke dion du. *See how I will carry this gun on the shoulder.*

yeen (v) return, go home; an order to "go back" to where one has come
e.g. Yeen aranghaquo/Seeng yeeen aranghaquo. *Go home now.*
(adj) a little; a bit
e.g. Ikpain i normi yeen aranghaquo. *Life is a bit better now.*

yeenee (v) lean on; place one's weight on; wedge against
e.g.1. Kpara yeenee nne a baikait. *Don't lean on my body.*
2. Unan u yeenee a kainaii. *A stone has wedged against a tree.*

yeeng (v) find, has found (something new); discover, discovered e.g. Ini nyini, ameme omi or yeeng iyik a enyi a urum a kormborm. *Once, my father found elephant tusks in the jungle.*

yep (v) stalk, follow quietly to hunt or catch; imitate; mimick; emulate

e.g. Ata utaip quor or ror u yep chaap. *That hunter knows how to stalk an animal.*

yeh (v) shout or bark at; warn, caution; admonish, reprimand, reproach

yene (v) lean something

e.g. Yene kemet kor ma. *Lean that fuelwood here.*

yeu (v) cross; walk or run past someone; pass, passed, over (eg. time)

e.g. 1. A ka keme u yeu orkpa quor. *Will you be able to cross that river?*

2. N ka nwei yeu ngo. *I will run past you.*

3. Or ka yeu uromo umorng. *He/she will passed his/her exams.*

yeye (v) shout at (briefly or once)

e.g. Yeye kwen quor ko or tire kaichim kor. *Shout at that child so that he/she stops that noise.*

yhion (n) hill, mountain

yiaang (n) a tree pangolin

yin (v) wrap up oneself or someone (especially with clothes or hands)

yina (v) wrap up (usually oneself or someone, especially with clothes or hands)

yini (v) following someone about (usually without giving him/her any breathing space)

e.g. A yini nning mmi ndai a baikait, ngo kwen quo? *Why are you following me about like this, you this child?*

yire (v) insist; egg on

yirere (v) lengthen (e.g rope); elongate, stretch out (e.g. neck)

yiri (adj) long (always precided by a noun, pronoun and/or an adverb)

e.g. Enu chor e nekere yiri. *That snake is really long.*

yiriri (adv) steadily and quietly, gently

e.g. 1. Or seeng yiriri ngha enu. *He/she moves steadily and quietly like a snake.*

(v) tingle; tingling

e.g. N keri enu baikait baimi be yiriri. *When I*

look at a snake my body tingles.

yiri yiri (adj) long

e.g. 1. M borngi akam a ikpain i yiri yiri. *I pray for long life.*

2. N kwaka kainaii kai yiri yiri. *I need a long stick.*

Yises (n) Jesus

yiiuut (n) a water chevrotain

yoi (v) shake (especially the waist); wave (e.g. the hand); dangle, swing, sway; hang down

e.g. 1. Yoi koonun kaingo. *Shake your waist.*

2. Yoi ibor bu chaang Orborn obon. *Wave your hands for our chief.*

yome (v) wander about

yonene (v) turn round; go round something

e.g. Yonene katana kor. *Turn round the other way.*

yonene (v) turn, turn round; rotate; revolve (oneself or something once)

1. Yonene kaik. *Turn round and go.*

2. Ntak a yonene kawat kor a? *Why did you rotate that hoop?*

yoonene (v) spin, spin round; turn, turn round; rotate (someone or something else)

yooni (v) spin, spin round; turn, turn round; turn around, revolve; rotate

e.g. 1. Kpara yooni ko etong a bai kuba ngo. *Don't spin round so you don't feel dizzy.*

2. Kwen quo or ya u yooni a doronghi daimi. *That child is fond of turning around in my backyard.*

3. Kaibain ke tireri u yooni. *The earth does not cease to rotate.*

yoonini (v) spin, spinning; rotate, rotating, revolve, revolving

e.g. Nke a durau, n na ning arangha kaibain ke yoonini. *Even in my wildest dreams, I have not seen how the earth is rotating.*

yoora (v) leaking

e.g. Enor engo e yoora kpai. *Your house is leaking too much.*

yoorni (v) yawn

yoornini (v) yawning

e.g. A yoornini mmung? *Why are you yawning?*

yoorp (v) deceive someone (usually into trouble)

e.g. A kemeni u yoorp orne ngha mmi. *You can't deceive someone like me into trouble.*

yoot (v) drip; leak

e.g. 1. Mini mu nka yoot a ntak a kotom kor ke chorm doboki. *The water will drip because the container has a hole.*

2. Enor engo e ka yoot na enaba chai. *Your house will leak this rainy season.*

yorkere (v) change; replace

e.g. 1. Seeng de yorkere eta aingo. *Go and change your clothes.*

2. Mbork, yorkere mmi inaii nyi. *Please, change me this money.*

3. A chorm u yorkere orairio quo, ntak or noormi. *You should replace this radio because it is not working.*

yorn (v) coil; twist, interweave

yoror (v) move up and down; perambulate, stroll; pay regular visits to; pace-dance (i.e. this way and that way, up and down as an ekwe masquerade does, in a dramatic manner)

e.g. 1. A yoror kwaka mmung? *What are you looking for moving up and down?*

2. Mmung a yoror enor chai nyi dai? *Why are you visiting this house like this, so regularly?*

3. Dibo di re kerei kai ke ror u yoror. *Dibo is a masquerade that knows how to pace-dance.*

yowoo! (inj) an expression of misfortune or sad news

yoya (v) shake; wave; wag (e.g. the tail)

e.g. 1. Kporkpora ini or kwaka u kaik, ta o yoya nne ubor. *Each time he/she is about to go, he/she waves me his/her hand.*

2. Kporkpora ini ebia chai e ning nne ta e yoya daikain demorng. *Each time this dog sees me it wags its tail.*

yui (v) stir (by turning with a stick)

yuui (v) call out aloud; to hoot (repeatedly)

yuya (v) call out aloud, hoot (once or momentarily)

yurere (v) twist (especially the arm)

e.g. Kpara a yurere ubor a kwen kwor. *Don't twist that child's arm.*

yurere maba (v) skrew (briefly)

e.g. Yurere maba duuni dor. *Screw that bottle top.*

yurere mabi (v) unscrew (briefly)

e.g. Yurere mabi duuni dor. *Unscrew that bottle top.*

yut (v) stir (by turning with a stick or spoon); screw; steer, turn (e.g. a steering)

yut maba (v) skrew (continually)

e.g. Yut maba duuni dor. *Screw that bottle top.*

yut mabi (v) unskrew (continually)

e.g. Yut mabi duuni dor. *Unscrew that bottle top.*

www.ingramcontent.com/pod-product-compliance
Lightning Source LLC
Chambersburg PA
CBHW021950290426
44108CB00012B/1012